TAKING POWER BACK

"Simon Parker offers substantive examples from the UK and elsewhere about how to achieve a lasting shift of power to cities, towns and local neighbourhoods. It is an ambitious but persuasive programme."

Peter Riddell, Director, Institute for Government

"Thought-provoking insights of what needs to change within our political and public services architecture, useful and challenging ideas about how we do that and the likely consequences if we don't."

Peter Holbrook, Chief Executive, Social Enterprise UK

"A timely and comprehensive case for devolution, helping to put the case for change in a way that is meaningful to people's daily lives. All in government – central and local – should read this book and act on it."

Sir Albert Bore, Leader, Birmingham City Council

"A compelling case that the British experiment with centralism has failed. Using examples from across the globe, this provocative book shows how a happier, healthier and more equal society can be built from the bottom up."

Graham Allen, MP

TAKING POWER BACK

PUTTING PEOPLE IN CHARGE OF POLITICS

Simon Parker

First published in Great Britain in 2015 by

Policy Press
University of Bristol
1-9 Old Park Hill
Bristol BS8 1SD
UK
t: +44 (0)117 954 5940
pp-info@bristol.ac.uk
www.policypress.co.uk
www.press.uchicago.edu

North American office:
The Policy Press
c/o The University of Chicago Press
1427 East 60th Street
Chicago, IL 60637, USA
t: +1 773 702 7700
f: +1 773 702 9756
sales@press.uchicago.edu

British Library Cataloguing in Publication Data
A catalogue record for this book is available from the British Library

Library of Congress Cataloging-in-Publication Data
A catalog record for this book has been requested

ISBN 978-1-4473-2687-8 paperback

Cover design by Soapbox Design
Printed and bound in Great Britain by TJ International,
Padstow.
Policy Press uses environmentally responsible print partners.

Contents

Acknowledgements

Some books are the unique product of a single mind. Most are a synthesis of many people's thoughts and experiences, and the name on the cover is simply that of the person who has written those ideas down as a coherent argument. This is a book of the latter sort. I run a think-tank that works with many of the most interesting thinkers and doers in the devolution debate; they are the lightning and my job is to act as a rod to channel their energy. With that in mind, I want to thank the members and staff of the New Local Government Network (NLGN) for the huge amount of support and inspiration they have given me over the past five years. I cannot possibly list them all by name, so will have to hope that they know who they are. I am particularly grateful to my chair, Jane Roberts, and her colleagues on the NLGN board for allowing me to work part time in order to get the book finished.

This project would not have happened without Terry Clague of Routledge, who believed in the original idea and pointed me in the direction of Policy Press. The initial proposal was heavily shaped by feedback from James Worron, a man with whom I disagree about almost everything of significance, but whose comments transformed my idea of what the book ought to be. My peer reviewers also played a big role in shaping the project. Thanks to Colin Copus, Daniel Goodwin, Jason Kitcat, Catherine Staite, Barry Quirk, Jon Wilson and Anthony Zacharzewski for their excellent feedback. Policy Press has also been hugely supportive, giving me precisely the right mix of space and support. My thanks to Alison Shaw and Laura Vickers for all their help and patience.

Andy Chapman bravely read the first five chapters at a time when they were barely fit for human consumption, and offered insightful comments and suggestions. George Jones allowed me to draw on his extraordinary wealth of knowledge. Matthew Pike pointed me in the direction of collective action methodology and Mark Walton put me on to Bologna. Neil McInroy receives a special mention for sending me comments that were, characteristically, both intellectually astute and very funny. Joost Beundermann, James Binks, Richard Blyth, Liam Booth-Smith, Adrian Brown, Tony Clements and Steve Skelton also provided useful comments. Many very busy people generously made time for interviews. Thanks to Clive Betts, Dan Corry, Michele D'Alena, Mike Emmerich, Christian Iaione, Sir Richard Leese, Geoff Little, Geoff Mulgan, Nick Raynsford and Graham Stringer.

I am indebted to the anonymous author of the Municipal Dreams blog, an outstanding collection of essays on the golden age of local government. Their work played a huge part in inspiring and informing the chapter on the history of localism. Heather Jameson helped make that chapter worthwhile by giving me the run of the archives at the *Municipal Journal*. I am indebted in a different sense to the staff of my local Café Rouge, who allowed me to use their restaurant as an office. This book is powered by their coffee and steak frites.

I am endlessly grateful to Alec for his patience with his busy dad, and to Cherry both for her love and for her suggestion that writing a book might be a good idea. The most important source of material for this text is our eight years of conversation about how to create a better politics.

Simon Parker
April 2015

Preface

This book is about the failure of a grand experiment with political power. It describes how one of the most decentralised countries in the world became the polar opposite in the course of a single lifetime. It shows how Britain's national politicians have desperately tried to assert their waning authority over a changing society, and it explains how their attempts at top-down control became expensive, ineffective and, ultimately, counterproductive. Today, it seems unlikely that we could maintain the status quo even if we wanted to: British centralism has come under assault from Celtic nationalism, budget cuts, new technology and changing social attitudes. Faced with such a powerful array of decentralising forces, the centre cannot hold.

The battle between the forces that would hoard power and those that would share is raging across the world. In America and across Europe, it has become commonplace to observe that cities have become vibrant and innovative at precisely the same time as national parliaments are becoming gridlocked. Examples in this book show how local political leaders and community groups in areas as diverse as New York and Bogota, Reykjavik and Tirana have seized the initiative and started to fix government from the ground up.

But while there are examples of positive change everywhere, the battle to decentralise power has become particularly potent in Britain. The 2015 election and its aftermath suggest that the political class is finally starting to grapple with the scale of change in the world outside Westminster. The Labour Party has finally begun a debate about its fatal addiction to high-powered paternalism. Far more significantly, David Cameron used his first speech at the head of a majority government to promise devolution to England's big northern cities.

It is important to be clear about what is really on offer. The conurbations of the Northern Powerhouse are winning more control over their economies and the right to work with central government to redesign healthcare and the skills system. This seems dangerously radical to some commentators, but the citizens of most other wealthy countries would wonder what all the fuss was about. The fatal flaw in the Conservative plans is that they do not include a penny of devolved responsibility for taxation. Cities can redesign their public services, but they have no say over how they are funded. This is devolution of the very tamest sort.

There is also a real danger that the Northern Powerhouse becomes a closed discussion between local and national elites, with the general public left out of the equation altogether. The creation of a Boris Johnson-style mayoralty for Greater Manchester should be the beginning of a conversation about power and democracy, not the end. Cities need to invite their citizens in to the closed world of local politics to hack the way that government works, not just replicate national power-hoarding at a local level.

National politicians like to claim they are winning power to give it away, but you cannot give away something that was never yours in the first place. Power exists in the relationships between ordinary people; it is a renewable force which we can generate for ourselves and our ability to do that is vastly amplified by the emergence of the networked society. Westminster too often tries to crush these forms of networked power, to a great extent because doing so leaves a larger gap for national politics to fill. It is high time we stopped letting them get away with it.

Across the world, ordinary people are starting to make change happen. From England's community pubs to the explosion of the cooperative movement and the anarchist disaster relief workers of Occupy Sandy, we are surrounded by reminders of how powerful civic activism can be. If there is a way out of our current political malaise, it lies in the creation of a radically enabling sort of government which creates the space for practical community entrepreneurship to thrive.

Prometheus has been tied to his rock for too long. It is time to unbind him. It is time to take power back.

Simon Parker
July 2015

ONE

The revolution will not be centralised: why top-down politics won't survive the 21st century

> If you want to drive through systemic change, you've got to drive it through from the centre. (Tony Blair, 2010[1])

> The objection to public ownership, in so far as it is intelligent, is in reality largely an objection to over-centralisation. (R.H. Tawney, 1920[2])

> Liberty without socialism is privilege, injustice; and socialism without liberty is slavery and brutality. (Mikhail Bakunin, 1867[3])

> Politics is going to be dominated by those with ideas about dispersing power. (Douglas Carswell, 2011[4])

The Millbank Tower is an unremarkable building. Once the tallest in London, it has long since been dwarfed by the skyscrapers to the east and south. These days, it is famous as a former Labour Party campaign headquarters and the site of some spectacular student rioting. But in the late 2000s, the first floor of the tower was occupied by a remarkable institution. The Audit Commission existed for a little over 30 years, during which time it grew from a financial watchdog for local public services into an all-encompassing empire of inspection.

For a time, this grey slab by the Thames became the nerve centre for British centralism, home to an organisation that spent over £200 million a year on assessing and counting what was happening in the country's town halls and reporting it all back to Whitehall. The Audit Commission was the emblem of a far larger command-and-control state that attempted to measure and manage everything from herbarium specimens to the level of meat eaten by the general public.[5] The Commission finally shut its doors in 2015, but do not let its empty offices fool you: the attitudes and institutions that underpin British statism are alive and well.

Modern governments seldom leave behind a physical record of their follies. There are few shattered visages lying in the desert to remind us of where things went wrong. The great, bleak council estates of the 1960s and 1970s have mostly been consigned to the past, many of them knocked down to make room for expensive new private housing. The Millennium Dome might once have counted, but it has been reinvented as one of the country's most successful music venues. Today's relics of ministerial hubris are failed IT projects, expensively discarded organisational structures and the abandoned premises of once-mighty quangos; failed attempts to use the brute force of the central state to tame and order a complex world.

This book is about power, and how politicians misunderstood its nature. Instead of seeing power as something that is spread across society, that lives in relationships and that can be activated only through motivating and persuading, our leaders have come to view it as something to be hoarded and directed. Over the past 70 years they have taken more and more control into their own hands, to the extent that Britain has become arguably the most centralised country in the developed world. Power is habit forming and, like most addictions, this one requires the user to take more and more to get the same effect, leaving its victims exhausted. The results are plain to see: inequality, permanent austerity, creaking public services and a democracy that leaves most of us feeling like bystanders. The only way out is for ministers to kick the habit: stop hoarding power and start sharing it with the country's cities, communities and with individual citizens. In doing so, they can empower people to help build a new country that is happier, more equal and more prosperous.

There was a time when Britain was one of the most decentralised nations in Europe. In the 1930s, local authorities ran swathes of hospital care and power generation and had a major stake in the benefits system as well as some aspects of education. Welfare was largely administered by the voluntary sector, with a strong emphasis on mutual aid and self-help. But by the 1990s, almost all these functions had been subsumed into the Whitehall machine and the highways of power had been rearranged so that they all led back to politicians at the centre. Today, central government controls about 91 pence of every pound raised in tax, more than in any other industrialised nation.[6] None of this was inevitable: other countries have built strong welfare states and weathered economic crises, social change and political conflict, yet only in Britain have we seen such a sustained and unremitting flow of powers and functions towards the centre.

Despite the 2010 Coalition government's promises to devolve, David Cameron and Nick Clegg did remarkably little to fundamentally reverse the trend towards the centre. In his first flush of power, Cameron promised regular progress reports on decentralisation. When the first one was released, it admitted that many departments still had a lot further to go, especially in terms of devolving control of public money and making services accountable to local people.[7] Unsurprisingly, no further reports were published. Even Cameron's most decentralising reform – allowing parents to set up their own free schools – is actually a way to remove many of local government's powers to regulate the school system and hand them to the Education Secretary. It remains to be seen whether a majority Conservative government can do any better with its promises to create a devolved 'Northern Powerhouse', handing new power to Manchester and the other great northern cities.

Like many other political leaders, Cameron and Clegg discovered that the very act of centralising power makes it hard to give away again. When national politicians promise to use central power to solve society's problems, or to address postcode lotteries, the public expects them to deliver. Once power is taken from councils or communities, their capacity to take it back can rapidly atrophy.

You might argue that none of this matters as long as central control delivers results. Surely the whole point of giving more power to ministers in London is to ensure equality? Yet Britain remains one of the most unequal countries in the developed world. An NHS run from Whitehall to ensure fairness has in fact presided over widening health inequalities, to the extent that the gap in premature deaths between rich and poor is now wider than during the Great Depression of the 1930s.[8] Centrally driven housing policy has consistently failed to build enough properties to meet growing need. Centrally managed skills policy has resulted in a mismatch between qualifications and jobs, symbolised by the vast oversupply of hairdressers and beauty technicians, when many firms need engineers and computer scientists.

This is before we even get into questions about the role of overly centralised and secretive policy making in such debacles as the poll tax, NHS reorganisation, benefits reform and the decision to go to war in Iraq. As professors Anthony King and Ivor Crewe point out, our model of government is not held up as an international exemplar any more, for the simple reason that 'today's British governments screw up so often'.[9] It is not that the central state is useless or bad, but that it too often overreaches itself, applying its powerful but blunt instruments to problems that it is ill-equipped to address.

This has contributed to a crisis of trust in politics: in 1986, 38% of us trusted the government to put the needs of the nation first; today that figure is just 17%.[10] Our political masters keep trying to find a convincing response. If only we could leave Europe and control our borders, we would finally be free. If only we stick to our plans to reduce the deficit, we will return to solid economic growth. If only we take on the banks and energy companies, we can create a fairer society. But what if the real challenge is the fact that we have allowed national politicians to become too mighty?

1 How new power is changing old politics

Power is simply the ability to make things happen in the world. The sociologist Manuel Castells defines it as 'the relational capacity that enables a social actor to influence asymmetrically the decisions of other social actors in ways that favour the empowered actor's will, interest and values'.[11] The point is that power lies in relationships, and in the networked society the nature of relationships is changing. They are far less structured by things like religions, clubs, political parties and trade unions. Instead, they are becoming far more fluid and horizontal. This is why we are currently witnessing the beginnings of a confrontation between two very different understandings of power. It is a confrontation that is particularly sharp in Britain, but which can also be seen playing out across the globe. Over the coming pages we will visit its frontlines, exploring how new approaches are emerging from Maryland to Tirana, and from Reykjavik to Bogota and Bologna. Where overly powerful central governments are reaching the limits of their ability to improve their societies, local institutions and citizens themselves are stepping into the breach.

On one side of the battle we have the *old power* of governments and big business. It relies on authority, hierarchy, professionalism and secrecy. It is essentially the power of laws, regulations, spending and bureaucracy. It can be very effective. The minimum wage is a good example: this is something that a government can legislate for and enforce that makes a real difference to people's lives. One survey of political scientists showed that they thought the minimum wage was the most successful policy intervention of the past 30 years, followed by devolution to Scotland and Wales and the privatisation of the nationalised industries.[12] None of these was easy to deliver, but they were all things that could be captured in bills and enforced in courts. The crooked timber of humanity is not so easily managed.

On the other side, we have what might be termed *new power*,[13] which is drawn from the relationships between people and relies on connectivity, openness and a willingness to collaborate for at least short spaces of time. It is good for mobilising people. If governments and big business typify old power, then we can find the newer sort at work in organisations like Wikipedia, the crowdfunding website Kickstarter and the Occupy movement. These are platforms upon which many people can work together to play out their hopes and dreams, writing, funding and protesting in a myriad of flexible ways. These organisations have their limitations. It is hard to imagine a world in which Kickstarter can replace the hierarchical authority necessary to run a police force. New power certainly cannot guarantee that everyone in the country gets a consistently good health service. But it is not so hard to imagine a similar kind of platform replacing large parts of the social care system. Indeed, it is already starting to happen.

Of course, new power is not really all that new. There is a sense in which it is a technologically driven rediscovery of the self-help ethos found in cooperatives and friendly societies in the era before the welfare state. The cooperative pioneer Robert Owen would have grasped the idea intuitively, and he would likely have recognised its potential to link people together in networks of mutual aid. Many of the latest developments in areas like education can trace their way back to thinkers from the 1970s such as Ivan Illich, who argued that society should be 'de-schooled' and that education should happen everywhere for anyone who wanted it.[14] He would have loved the massively open online courses that are disrupting university education by allowing students across the world to learn from the best professors at Harvard and Cambridge in their lunch hours.

Neither is new power inherently virtuous. The taxi company Uber, for instance, provides an alternative to minicab services by using an app to link together drivers and passengers. The middle men are cut out and the barriers to becoming a cab driver are lowered, resulting in cheaper rides. But Uber makes its money partly by undermining the old power of existing cab drivers, who lose the premium they can charge because of their superior training. It is busting open a very old closed shop, but the company has become mired in questions about its tax affairs, its attitude to women and the fact that it temporarily hiked its prices during a terrorist attack in Sydney. One journalist recently asked whether Uber might be the worst company in Silicon Valley.[15] It is using new-power methods, but many people argue that it is coupling them with old-power values.

The point is not that new power must replace old power; it is that a new balance needs to be found between the old forces of hierarchy and the new opportunities of a networked world. Look at the way that the music industry has dealt with the challenge of internet file sharing. First it attempted to enforce its old business model by trying to shut down file-sharing sites and prosecuting people who share music. This simply made the record labels unpopular. Then it innovated. Music became a way to sell merchandise and tours, then streaming services like Spotify provided a legal way to monetise file sharing. The industry adapted and a new synthesis began to emerge.

Our politicians are becoming like the music companies that tried to crack down on Napster, but without the commercial pressure that forced transformation upon Sony and EMI. The parties are stuck in an old-power rut and cannot see a way to integrate new power into their work. The problem for politicians is that the more power they gather to themselves in the world of hierarchy, the less credibility they have in the network. To put it simply, taking on more power does not always make you more powerful. Centralism overloads politicians, creates unrealistic expectations of what they can achieve for their voters and encourages hubris. At its worst, this can create a vicious cycle in which every time something goes wrong in a council or hospital, the public demands that something must be done and ministers are forced to take on more power to intervene, entrenching the perception that the answer to any problem lies in action from Westminster.

We live in the midst of a decade of public spending cuts that will fundamentally reshape the social state. Unless the current political consensus on austerity somehow changes, the UK government will soon be spending a substantially smaller proportion of national wealth on public services. With health, education and international development likely to be at least partially protected from cuts, the axe will fall heavily on areas like policing, social services for children and the elderly and the funding the government puts into infrastructure and supporting economic growth. This represents perhaps the biggest shift in the role of the British state since 1945. The post-war history of public services is an interrupted

and uneven pattern of expansion as the range of provision for
healthcare, education and the elderly grew to meet the needs of
an expanding population and a post-industrial economy. Now, for
the first time, we face the prospect of a permanent reduction in
the scope of government action, driven both by the need to pay
off the deficit and by the huge costs associated with our ageing
population.

The post-war welfare settlement is dying. The only real question
is what will come next. Will it be a world of creaking public
services focused on the very poorest, or can we harness the
potential of new power to create a new approach to supporting
each other, based on mutualism? Can we imagine a progressive
approach to politics and society that combines the state's power
to regulate and redistribute with the network's power to unlock
social action? If this approach is going to work, we are going to
need equivalents of Kickstarter for social care, enabling all of us
to play a part in caring for older people. We are going to need to
work together to maintain parks and grit side roads. We are going
to need to form local trusts to maintain our own parks and green
spaces. Ultimately, we are going to have to find a new balance
between the role of the state, communities and the private sector.
It is nigh-on impossible to imagine doing this while maintaining
the current, over-centralised structure of the British state.

2 The mimes that transformed a city

What would a shift in our understanding of politics to encompass
new power really look like? The simple truth is that no one knows,
because no one has done it yet. But it is possible to make some
educated guesses by contrasting two very different leaders from
the recent past.

In 1999, Tony Blair summoned a group of academics and
economists to Toynbee Hall, a settlement house developed in the
19th century to minister to the poor of East London. It was a bright
March morning in the days when his Labour government still felt
new and exciting, and the announcement that Blair made was of
a piece with that early optimism: his government would abolish

child poverty within a generation. 'It is a 20 year mission, but I believe it can be done', the Prime Minister said.[16] The problem was that Blair was a classic old-power politician. Rather than grasp the opportunity to swing the whole might of the public sector behind his pledge, engaging communities and local people in a crusade to end poverty, Blair came forward with changes to benefits and support into work. What might have been a social crusade against the scourge of child poverty was turned into a series of technical changes and financial transfers.

It did not work. Blair set a target of halving child poverty by 2010. Labour made progress, but when the deadline came it was still 600,000 away from hitting the goal.[17] Not enough parents had moved into work, or progressed in their jobs. The jobs that parents did get often did not pay very well, so some families simply exchanged unemployed poverty for in-work poverty. Eradicating child poverty, it turned out, would need much wider changes to the way power and opportunities were distributed across society. The child poverty target was perhaps the single most defining pledge of the New Labour years, both in terms of its sheer progressive ambition and in terms of the gap between the soaring goal and the quotidian bureaucratic reality. As Blair discovered, and as Iain Duncan Smith's experience reminds us, you cannot transform a society by tinkering with its benefits system.

In 1993, a very different sort of leader won the mayoralty in the Colombian city of Bogota. Antanas Mockus was not what most people would regard as prime political material. A slightly awkward academic who lived with his mother, his national profile rested on his decision earlier that year to drop his trousers and wiggle his bottom to a crowd of protesting students. The incident happened live on national television. It silenced the crowd, but it cost Mockus his job as president of Bogota University. It also made him look refreshingly different from the corrupt party politicians who usually carved up the city's politics.[18]

Mockus would spend his term turning Bogota into an experiment in political philosophy. He believed that the only way to transform what was then an extremely violent city was to educate the public, changing their beliefs and culture in order to change their behaviour. He would state that: 'The distribution of knowledge is the key contemporary task. Knowledge empowers people. If people know the rules, and are sensitized by art, humour, and creativity, they are much more likely to accept change.'

The result was a series of beautiful, creative stunts. Mockus wanted to reduce homicide in Bogota, so he started by targeting traffic deaths. He worked out that traffic jams at major junctions were often caused by people pushing their way into queues rather than waiting their turn. So he distributed red and white cards allowing drivers to show their approval or disapproval of each other's behaviour, creating a form of self-regulation that allowed the traffic to flow more easily. He put up boards carrying images of traffic police at busy junctions, with the head cut out so that anyone could direct traffic without the drivers knowing if they were a traffic cop or not.

Mockus' next step was to move away from the city's ineffectual system of fining bad drivers; he decided to make fun of them instead. He hired a troupe of mime artists that would become 420 strong, fanning out across the city's most dangerous junctions to mock irresponsible motorists, stop traffic to allow it to flow more safely and playfully lead pedestrians over crossings. Films of the time show white-faced mimes fearlessly leaping in front of mini vans and fruitlessly attempting to push them back across packed junctions until the driver finally engages his reverse gear and backs up. It turns out to be surprisingly hard to summon up road rage against a clown.

It was the early 1990s and the internet was in its infancy, but Mockus was clearly experimenting with a form of new power. He reasoned that by giving people information, helping them to understand the effects of their actions on others, and giving them the authority to act, he could help them to transform the city for themselves. It worked. Traffic fatalities fell by more than half, homicide fell by over 70% and 63,000 of the city's residents voluntarily paid an extra 10% in tax to fund public services. All of this can sound ridiculous to sceptical Anglo-Saxon ears, but the truth is that a similar understanding of power as something that resides in the citizenry, not the state, can be found at the root of our current welfare state. We have come to think of the 1945 settlement as the beginning of an era of big government, but many of the people who shaped the welfare state were profoundly sceptical about the ability of state action alone to transform society.

3 The devolutionaries

William Beveridge would likely have anticipated a health service run by local authorities, not controlled from Whitehall, and a benefits system with a substantial role for voluntary friendly societies. His friend R.H. Tawney, the patron saint of the inter-war Labour movement, became disillusioned with a welfare settlement that he felt had made the working classes richer but had failed to morally transform Britain. Sidney and Beatrice Webb had once made the case that many functions of government should be municipalised, rather than nationalised. Michael Young, an author of Labour's 1945 manifesto, would leave his job with the party and plunge into a life of social activism outside government. For these men and women, organisations such as the Consumers' Association, the Workers' Educational Association and the Open University were at least as important as the new welfarism. Their most obvious heirs in modern politics are the circle of MPs and thinkers around Labour's Jon Cruddas.[19]

The root of much of this thinking lies with a generation of barely remembered anti-authoritarian Victorian radicals like William Morris,[20] a bearlike figure who these days is best known for the sumptuous wallpapers he designed to decorate middle-class sitting rooms. But Morris was also a firebrand socialist whose books included homages to John Ball, the preacher who inspired the Peasants' Revolt – and lost his head for it. Morris's was a socialism that seems very odd to modern eyes, but that was influential in its day. His political masterpiece was a book entitled *News from Nowhere*, in which a Victorian socialist falls asleep and awakens in a utopian future in which the people have turned away from consumerism and live in a sort of idealised medieval paradise. This being Morris, one of the first things our time traveller notices is the workmanship of his interlocutor's 'beautifully wrought' belt buckle.[21] In this world, art and culture reign supreme, society is run by groups of self-governing artisans and parliament has been turned into a dung store, a use Morris clearly believed to be more valuable than the political debate of his day.

The decentralising tendency is, if anything, more pronounced in the Conservative tradition. The 19th-century Tory radical Joshua Toulmin-Smith famously founded a group known as the Anti-Centralisation Union, based on his belief in the virtue of local self-government. A famous Tory election poster from 1929 shows a group of official inspectors poking their long noses into the home of a concerned looking Englishman. The slogan reads: 'Socialism would mean inspectors all round. If you want to call your soul your own, vote Conservative.' The heirs of this tradition on the Right are men like Douglas Carswell, for whom technology offers an opportunity radically to scale back the big state and devolve massive power to cities and individuals. You can even find a strand of localism among free-marketeers like the TaxPayers' Alliance, who want cities to control their own finances so that they can compete with one another to lower tax bills. The anti-state traditions of Left and Right are very different indeed in their motivations and their hopes for the future, but both agree that a more decentralised world would be a better one.

This is a very old part of our political tradition, only temporarily eclipsed by the long half-life of the post-war welfare settlement, but it is one that is coming to the fore once again. Recent polls show that 69% of the British public distrust big business and 71% distrust big government.[22] This is not very surprising. The 2008 financial crisis demonstrated that large banks could not be trusted with the very high levels of economic power they had gathered to themselves. The result was a financial crisis that was solved only with massive increases in public spending, tipping the country into a public debt crisis. Both the state and the market have failed us. If the choice is between being cosseted by government or crushed by market forces, many of us have decided we want neither.

The alternative is to bring power closer to ordinary people, partly by vesting more of it in local institutions that voters can really influence, but also by engaging citizens themselves more in everything from healthcare to housebuilding. Rather than building better public services, we have a historic opportunity to build a better society by sharing power. A burgeoning global movement is beginning to articulate a new vision of a civic commons – a world in which people take over and collaboratively manage valuable resources and services that we all use but nobody owns. For commoners, a smaller state might not be a bad thing as long as we also have a smaller private sector. The gap must be filled with a vibrant social sector characterised by local participation and shared management.

For centralised, statist Britain this amounts to a revolutionary idea. We tend to think local issues are dull, but we all live in a neighbourhood and a community that is the site of many of our hopes and dreams and that plays a huge part in forging the relationships that are so vital to our personal happiness. National change is worthwhile only to the extent that it improves our everyday lives and, at a time when centralised politics is so heavily distrusted, radical thinkers from across the globe are seeking salvation and innovation in local movements for change. In fact, a common language of utopia is starting to emerge, demanding a society that, in the words of the writer Rebecca Solnit, is 'less authoritarian and fearful, more collaborative and local'.[23]

Seen in this light, a call for decentralisation is much more than a demand that the deckchairs be rearranged on the sinking ship of the British state: it is a plea for a different approach to politics, one where we as citizens are not the passive recipients of Whitehall's largesse, but active creators of our own destiny. A call for decentralisation is a demand for a different way of doing government: one that argues that politics must do more to set the context in which good lives can be led, but less to enforce its own particular version of what that good life should be. In doing so, ministers can create the space for new power to flourish.

The underlying operating principle of the Blair administrations was simple: the market would grow and provide ever-expanding wealth, but it would also exclude some people. This meant that business should be encouraged to work with relatively little interference, producing surpluses that could be taxed to fund public services that would help to bring the excluded back into the fold. The result was a bossy and only somewhat effective series of governments. Not only did the market eventually stop growing, but public services proved unequal to the task of fixing the social problems that the market society generated. The Tory model is really just a much less generous version of Blair's. It too holds that the market should be left alone, but it also argues that there are reserves of self-reliance and social capital that will flourish if only the state withdraws.

The principles that underpin decentralisation offer a new operating model for 21st-century government. In this approach, government is much more concerned with ensuring that markets produce better outcomes in the first place, and much less concerned with picking up the costs of personal and social failure. This suggests two clear roles for a modernised Westminster government.

The first role is to create an economic context in which people can lead good lives. This does not mean 1970s-style industrial policies that prop up inefficient businesses with taxpayers' money, but it does mean actively shaping the economy to ensure that it creates fewer problems for government to solve. This needs to involve active policies to improve productivity, invest in innovation, increase pay, radically improve skills levels and ultimately create jobs that provide a route out of poverty. It also means much firmer action to build new housing, green the economy and build high-quality transport and energy infrastructures. Central government can do a certain amount to create the macro-economic conditions for growth, but it is far less effective at managing the micro-economic factors that make cities successful. That is precisely why we need to devolve micro-economic tools to the local level.

If the first critical role for government is in setting a good economic context for our lives, the second is in setting the social context. In the coming decade, this cannot be done simply by providing more and more state spending on public services; we do not have the money for that. Instead, it means that government must take on a key role in encouraging non-state, non-market forms of social action. If the state cannot do as much to keep our neighbourhoods healthy, clean and happy, then we will need to find new ways to help one another. We need politicians to support the creation of the commons through their leadership, by helping to provide funding and by putting their power and assets at ordinary people's disposal. Again, this is the kind of fine-grained work that is impossible to carry out from the heights of Whitehall.

The assault on centralism has already begun. It is an insurgency that can be found in Greater Manchester, where the city's 10 councils have come together to demand more control over their own destiny, wresting control of the city's urban fabric and public services away from the policy makers in Whitehall. The leaders of what has arguably become Britain's second city have started a clamour from their counterparts in Leeds, Newcastle and Sheffield for comparable powers, closely followed by the Tory shire counties. Similar forces can be seen at work in the cooperative movement, which surged by 26% from 2009 to 2013,[24] and in a new spirit of community activism. Just look at the number of communities coming together to set up their own renewable energy generation facilities, the libraries that have been redesigned so that local people can create their own books and make their own objects, not just consume things that others have made, and the apps that are encouraging people to cook dinner for their elderly neighbours. Then there is the new wave of volunteers taking control of threatened local services to save them from cuts. Local people have taken ownership of everything from an underground shop in Devon to a cinema in Northumberland.

The forces driving calls for power to be shared are becoming too powerful for our politicians to ignore. There has always been a strong case for saying that centralism is inefficient, but this is now being joined by a case for renewing democracy and allowing a far wider range of people to contribute their creative energies to the task of social change. Both big political parties have committed themselves to localism, in rhetoric if not always in reality. Their most substantial shared pledge is the idea of giving cities more control over their own urban planning, policing and skills, essentially allowing the northern metropolises to catch up with, and in some cases go beyond, the powers already granted to London's mayor. These are steps in the right direction, but they do not change anything fundamental about British governance. The money remains locked up in Whitehall and Westminster, as does control of the vast bulk of public services and spending. Ministers still feel within their rights to demand that councils pay individual staff members less and empty the bins more often.

The 45% of Scots who voted for independence did so not just so that they could run their own affairs, but so that they could create their own, better, style of politics. Independence was just a starting point. So it is with our cities. The public demand for change cannot be assuaged simply by shuffling a few powers between Whitehall and the board room of the Greater Manchester Combined Authority, between the big state and the slightly smaller state. As the Scottish experience shows, devolving power to another tier of administration is not a panacea. The Scottish government has proved to be highly centralising, effectively forcing a council tax freeze and a raft of prescriptive national targets onto local authorities. Gordon Matheson, the leader of Glasgow City Council, puts it well: 'True devolution isn't about transferring powers from one centralising government to another.'[25] The same is even more true of the case for English votes for English laws, a solution that devolves power from a governance unit of 64m people to one of 53m, which barely counts as decentralisation at all.

There is an anarchic spirit of community-driven change abroad in the land that is hugely valuable both in itself and as an anchor for a more decentralised approach to government. But it cannot take root in a system where power remains so centralised and bureaucratised. We need a much broader debate about the future of power in our society. In this book, I hope to start it.

The coming chapters answer four questions. How, and why, has the centralist experiment failed, how did the British come to undertake such a peculiar experiment in the first place and, most importantly, how might things be different if we abandoned it? Is it possible to imagine a decentralised way to govern Britain that can deliver better results in a world where there is much less money? As you will have worked out by now, I believe we face an array of urgent social questions that are too important to be left to the politicians to decide on their own. Power ultimately comes from the people: there has never been a better time for us to start using it.

4 The new politics of democratic republicanism

I have spent the past 15 years writing, debating and occasionally influencing the discussion about the future shape of Britain's cities and public services. I have been careful never to wield any sort of substantial power myself. At the turn of the century, I was one of the many thinkers who believed that we were witnessing a sort of end of history in the debate about the role of the state. The radicals on the Right had privatised the nationalised industries and driven up the efficiency of public services, but by 1997 their energy was spent. The Blair governments appeared to have created a consensus in favour of a state that spent something like 42% of GDP on services and accompanied that spending with big reforms to promote competition and choice between hospitals and schools. What mattered seemed to be about what government did, and how effectively it did it, not how much it spent.

Lord Kelvin famously declared that there was nothing new to be discovered in physics, just more and more precise measurement. This was how the mid- to late-Blair years felt to a lot of people, myself included. Kelvin was proved wrong, and so were we. The Blairite consensus was shattered by the financial crisis and, all of a sudden, our project of gradually improving public services was shown to be wholly inadequate. Big, troubling questions came back onto the debating table. How could we maintain public services at anywhere near the level we had become used to in a world where money was scarce and the problems facing government seemed to keep mounting? Were those public services really as good as we had thought they were, or were some parts of the public sector actually contributing to social problems by creating inefficiency and dependency? What did it mean to be a Leftist who felt increasingly sceptical about the ability of the big, centralised state to solve social problems?

This book is an attempt to describe a positive way forward. Its politics do not fit easily onto the traditional political spectrum.

Much contemporary left-wing political thought is anchored in a form of scientific socialism drawn from Marx and the Fabian tradition of Sidney and Beatrice Webb.[26] For these thinkers, the problem with capitalism is that it is unfair and inefficient; the remedy is a strong state that can redistribute wealth, regulate business and fund social programmes. But there is another strand of progressive thought that critiques the market from an ethical and aesthetic perspective: the problem with capitalism is that it constrains the human spirit and is therefore ugly. For this tradition, the purpose of politics is to liberate people to fulfil their creative potential. It is this strand of thinking that you will find reflected in the following pages. The argument is strongly in favour of progressive values and the achievement of better social outcomes, but deeply sceptical of the ability of either state centralism or the free market to achieve those goals, whether singly or in combination.

It is a politics that blends aspects of two philosophical traditions. The first is democratic republicanism, a strand of thinking that takes individual liberty as its starting point but insists that freedom is worthwhile only when it enables people to make real choices about their lives. For a liberal, it is enough that a slave should be left alone by their master to do as the slave pleases, but for a democratic republican, the very possibility that the slave could be told what to do is abhorrent. To be truly free, the slave needs to be liberated and helped to become autonomous in a society that does not allow the possibility of a return to servitude. The second tradition is William Morris's libertarian socialism, in which the point of the state is to provide the support necessary for individual flourishing, with its functions firmly subordinated to the individual and democratic will. Liberty is the ability to be the hero of your own life, and justice is a society in which this becomes possible for everyone.[27]

TWO

Learning to love the postcode lottery: why hoarding power usually fails

The postcode lottery is a surprisingly recent British obsession. Search through the archives and you will struggle to find many mentions of the idea before the late 1990s.[1] These days, however, you never have to wait long for a newspaper headline pointing out that some fortunate parts of the country are able to provide more regular bin collections, more effective cancer drugs or better levels of funding for the arts and the voluntary sector than others. The *Daily Mail* alone published 98 stories about postcode lotteries in 2014. How can it be fair that some people get better services than others? The answer is always the same: sensible, capable national politicians must take action to sort out the mess local professionals have made of their own services. Policies must be adopted and poor performers named and shamed. Control must be asserted, and if that doesn't work, then the answer is usually even more control. Centralism promises fairness and equality in place of senseless place-by-place variations. This sounds like basic common sense, but what if it isn't true at all?

In 2011, the Communities Secretary, Eric Pickles, took the stand at the annual conference of the think-tank that I run. He had come into office on a promise to devolve more power to local councils. Few of the people in the hall believed he had delivered. Nonetheless, Pickles thought he saw a major threat to localism on the horizon, and that threat was bin collections. Too many councils had decided to scrap weekly bin rounds to save money and increase recycling rates. The move to fortnightly collections 'fills middle England with rage',[2] said Pickles. The Communities

Department scrabbled together £250m of scarce government money and exhorted councils to take the cash and restore the weekly service. As the 2015 election loomed, not one council had responded and the Secretary of State was threatening to get his way through a new bins Bill.[3]

In 2014, a survey of clinical commissioning groups, the local organisations that decide how to spend public money on the NHS, showed that three-quarters of them were not following national guidance on hip replacements.[4] In some areas patients had to lose weight before getting the surgery, in others they had to already be in pain or immobilised. The answer on offer from the Royal College of Surgeons, which commissioned the survey, was more policy and regulation from the government.

In 2008, Haringey Council was rocked by the Baby Peter scandal, in which a toddler died after months of abuse. The scandal highlighted deep failings in the council's social services department and the media wanted someone to hold responsible. The then Children's Secretary, Ed Balls, intervened to demand that Sharon Shoesmith, the council's children's director, should be sacked. Six years later, the appeal court would rule that Shoesmith had been unfairly scapegoated, Balls was blamed for his role in her unlawful sacking and she received what was reportedly a six-figure compensation package.

Take any of these stories in isolation and the responses of the public, ministers and interest groups might seem entirely reasonable, if not always very effectual. But add them together with hundreds of other incidences of the postcode lottery and you find a deeply unhealthy spiral of centralism that drives ever more power and responsibility back into the hands of a few people in London.

Politicians come into power promising to make the country a better and fairer place. When things go wrong with our local services, the public and the media demand that ministers take action. The problem is that most of the tools at the government's disposal involve taking more central control of public services. Sometimes this is quite effective. The targets introduced by Tony Blair to ensure that all patients arriving at accident and emergency (A&E) departments were seen within four hours more or less worked, even if quite a few hospitals played fast and loose with the data. When public sector organisations fail, there is sometimes no option but for central government to step in and sort them out. But more often, when ministers take on more power they fail to solve the problem, and the next time the same problem emerges the government comes under ever more pressure to take on even more power.

Centralism is like Santa Claus: something almost no one really believes in, but which adults pretend is real whenever they want to placate, delight or punish the kids. To the extent that there is a coherent political philosophy behind the brute fact of top-down control, it usually comes down to equality. The argument is that only a battery of tightly enforced national targets and standards can ensure that the poor and vulnerable across the country receive fair treatment.[5] We can test this easily. If centralism leads to equality, then the increasing centralisation of British politics since the Thatcher era should have made the country at least a slightly fairer place. In fact, the precise opposite has happened. We currently have one of the highest levels of income inequality in Europe[6] and some of the lowest levels of social mobility.[7] Decentralised countries such as Germany and Denmark do better on both measures. The NHS is one of the most centralised public service systems in the world, and yet performance from place to place can be hugely variable.[8] If the goal is a fairer nation, central control is doing a lousy job of delivering it. Top-down control is not even very efficient, because it encourages the development of huge national projects which often go expensively wrong. A cursory glance at reports from the National Audit Office from 2006 to 2012 reveals more than £3.3bn of waste from tinkering at the centre, including £780 million simply for reorganising government departments and agencies.[9]

While it is obviously reasonable to expect a core set of entitlements that everyone should get no matter who they are or where they are, the longer that list gets, the harder, more bureaucratic and more expensive it becomes to enforce. A huge number of the goals and targets that governments set are simply missed. Only 40% of the targets that the Labour government set in its 2005 spending review were met,[10] and things did not improve greatly under the Coalition government's much less ambitious impact-indicator system. This set 207 areas in which departments were supposed to deliver improvements, but by the end of the last Parliament only 55% of the indicators were heading in the right direction. Only one department could show that it had delivered improvements on all of its indicators.[11] This leaves aside the question of whether those goals were the right ones if the first place.

Centralism clearly cannot deliver fairness or rid us of the postcode lottery, but its supporters might argue that without tight control from Whitehall the country would be in an even worse position. Here, too, they would be wrong. Emerging evidence suggests that decentralisation can make us richer, more equal and even happier. Analysis of data from across Europe shows that giving high levels of power to regions and localities tends to go hand in hand with higher levels of personal well-being. Far from making countries less fair, giving regions and cities more control of their own taxes has made poorer European regions more equal.[12] This may be because devolution can drive wealth creation, particularly when it includes tax-raising powers: more decentralised countries tend to have higher GDP per head of population,[13] and one recent study suggests that devolving more power over planning, transport and higher education to England's large cities outside London could add as much as £79bn to our GDP by 2030.[14] In statistical terms, some of these effects are stronger than others, but they are all real and they point in precisely the opposite direction to many of our concerns about the postcode lottery.

The spiral of centralism has reached such a profoundly unhealthy pitch that nearly three of out five Britons say they expect more from their politicians than they do from God.[15] The politicians themselves certainly recognise the problem. In a weary speech in 2003, former Home Secretary David Blunkett worried that he was expected to take responsibility for reducing crime when it was at least partly the job of an operationally independent police force.[16] What Blunkett did not mention was that he himself had played a role in creating those expectations. Dan Corry, a veteran of the Labour years who led Gordon Brown's Downing Street policy unit, highlighted much the same problem in an interview for this book:

> "The conceit of centralism is that a centralist lever will answer every problem. When ministers have that power they are under pressure to use that power, from local people, from the media who want some action, from Parliament. That becomes a crazy circle. You use it in ways that don't achieve anything, you can make it harder for local people to do the right thing and you get into a vicious circle."

Nick Raynsford, a veteran former Labour minister who held the briefs for London, housing and local government from 1997 to 2005, makes a similar point:

> "[Centralists seek to] achieve equality of outcomes across different areas even though there are huge inequalities of input. That's quite a difficult concept. You've got to have minimum standards, then give people the freedom to go beyond them. If you try and enforce the same outcomes everywhere, then you need a huge bureaucracy to manage and inspect."

It is not even clear that the public really wants all of this centralism. It is certainly true that 63% of us think that public services should be the same, no matter where you live,[17] but the same surveys show that the British can be persuaded to support very radical forms of devolution. For instance, nearly two-thirds of us say that if neighbourhoods take on more responsibility for addressing things like crime and anti-social behaviour, they should also take on some control of police budgets.[18] In other words, the public are open to persuasion from their leaders.

We do care about fairness, but we also care about local responsiveness. If you go to hospital and get seen within four hours, then that A&E department has hit its central government target. But that tells us nothing about whether you were treated with dignity and fairness, or whether you thought your treatment was actually any good. You can treat people as efficiently as you like, but if you fail to show them respect they are unlikely to thank you for it. There is a real tension here: force public servants to look up to Whitehall, and you reduce their capacity to look outwards to patients and citizens.[19] Central control cannot ensure that local people feel involved in decisions about their services, and yet satisfaction with both health and crime reduction is closely linked to whether or not the public have been effectively consulted and listened to.

Centralism is not uniquely responsible for the problems of British democracy. Nor is it uniquely to blame for the huge challenges facing our public services. It did not cause the banking crisis, the recession that followed it, nor the gigantic government deficit that followed the recession. Neither is the use of central control to be completely abjured – it clearly has its uses. But it is becoming increasingly clear that the extremely centralist path that the UK has followed for so long is no longer helping us to deal with a world in which our economy is sputtering, our politics is fragmenting and our town halls and hospitals face crippling cuts.

In fact, centrally controlled public services have managed to muddle the priorities of a number of vital policy areas to the extent that they are almost exactly back to front.

1 Why we spend more on gastric bands than losing weight

On a cold evening in 2014, with night and winter starting to creep over London, a group of trade union activists gathered opposite the House of Commons. They lit candles and stood there for hours waiting for the results of a vote on a Bill that would try to roll back the expanding role the private sector plays in the health service. It was one of those quasi-religious moments that symbolises the British attachment to the NHS. It is perhaps our most trusted national institution, containing our most trusted professionals in the saintly forms of doctors and nurses. It is very hard to imagine anyone pulling off a candle-lit vigil in defence of

Eric Pickles' weekly bin collections. And yet our very attachment to keeping the NHS as it currently is, resisting hospital closures and the encroachment of the private sector, is starting to blind us to the very real, very dangerous challenges facing the service over the coming decade.

The truth is that business is not the real enemy – the Department of Health says that only six pence in every pound of NHS money goes to the private sector, an increase of a penny since 2010. At this rate, it will take a very long time to privatise the NHS and, even if we did use the private sector more often, it is not obvious why a mixed economy is inherently such a bad thing as long as care remains free at the point of use.

The bigger issue is *us*. The British population is growing, ageing, adopting unhealthy habits and developing long-term conditions that cost more to treat. Historically, the NHS has coped by rationing care and waiting for more money to come along; the service has had an average of 4% more funding a year in real terms since vesting day in 1948.[20] If we assume that this is what the health service really needs to cope with rising demand, then hospitals and GPs face a funding gap of about £30bn[21] by the end of the decade, which can be filled only by a combination of pay freezes, huge efficiency savings and something like £8bn of new money. Look to the longer term, and the picture becomes even bleaker.

New technology can help by delivering better medicines and allowing more medical procedures to be carried out by GPs and nurses, reducing the pressure on very highly paid consultants. Experimenting with innovative new ways to combine technology with management reforms might yield even more benefits. But ultimately, if we want to maintain the NHS in anything like its current form, we are going to have to get ill less often and find better ways to manage our conditions when we do. The politicians have known this for a very long time. Labour commissioned a major review of the NHS in 2002 which showed that by far the most optimistic future for healthcare was one in which the public became far more engaged in keeping themselves healthy, supported by better access to health information and leading to a reduction in problems such as smoking and obesity.[22]

More than 10 years on, the verdict from health experts is that the job of reforming the NHS and engaging the public is 'very unfinished'.[23] While some areas of public health have improved dramatically – we smoke a lot less than we did 15 years ago – others have deteriorated significantly. The UK currently faces an epidemic of obesity, and alcohol is responsible for around 10 million hospital visits a year. The truth is that many of the factors that are driving poor health are not really the responsibility of the NHS at all. Doctors cannot stop us eating or drinking too much, driving everywhere rather than walking or failing to take exercise.

Analysis from the US suggests that only about 20% of the influences on our health are to do with clinical care. The rest is down to our own behaviour, our physical environment and our socio-economic background.[24] The way we manage healthcare in the UK does not reflect this fact. The NHS spends just 4% of its budget on preventing illness[25] and puts more money into fitting gastric bands than it does into programmes that have been proved to drive weight loss.[26] Outside of the A&E department, hospitals are paid for every patient they treat, not for every potential operation they prevent.

The centralised structure of the health service means that hospitals and GPs are overwhelmingly focused on treating people rather than avoiding the need for treatment in the first place. Ultimately, the health service is always likely to prioritise dealing with its regular winter flu crises over investing in stemming the sources of those crises. Many in the NHS are perfectly happy with this, because they believe the government will eventually bail them out. After all, that is what all preceding governments have done. The NHS has become too big to fail, and it knows it, but unless we find a way to restore the economy to very high levels of growth, the only way for the health service to get its money will be through higher taxes or cuts in other services.

A large part of the problem lies in Whitehall. The Department of Health is responsible for treatment, but the wider determinants of health are spread across the departments for Communities, Culture and Education. No one at central government level can bring them all together and, even if they could, it is hard to imagine how a department of state could manage the bewildering range of local relationships needed to coordinate a push on prevention. As one academic assessment of recent NHS policy puts it:

> NHS systems are about healthcare and (despite the name) departments of health are about the vast NHS systems that they oversee. This means that asking them to promote health, as against healthcare, is always difficult; their policy tools allow them to treat the sick, not tutor the healthy (or, less still, reduce inequality, improve workplace safety or reduce social exclusion).[27]

Ultimately, saving the NHS requires schools, councils and the health service to work together with the voluntary sector and business to redesign preventative healthcare. We need a shift from a national service focused on treatment to a localised service based on wellness, with a greater proportion of health service money finding its way into programmes for reducing youth obesity, growing locally produced food and encouraging physical activity. But this requires central government to let go of the levers of control. As Steve Bullock, the mayor of Lewisham, puts it, 'it is possible to envisage a system where the basic assumption is that keeping people out of hospital is what we aim to do',[28] but only if local places and local people take a bigger role in healthcare.

2 Why we spend more on subsidising rents than building new homes

Walk through Hulme these days, and you will encounter streets of red-brick terraces. These are the kind of houses you will find on the fringes of many urban centres; the classic Barratt estates. But not so long ago the streets of this part of Manchester were home to one of the greatest disasters in modern British housing policy. Hulme was the site of a gigantic council housing development known as the Crescents, a name which recalled the sweeping Georgian terraces of Bath, but which came to sound like a cruel joke.

It all started well. The Crescents were part of a much wider movement to clear Britain's slums of poor-quality housing and replace them with gleaming, modernist tower blocks. The houses that they replaced were often squalid; rapidly built to house Manchester's burgeoning working class, many lacked baths or laundry facilities. Hulme's new scheme was designed to provide good places to live, and to create a sense of community on the decks that provided access to the upper stories. The *Manchester Evening News* praised the way the plans brought 'a touch of eighteenth century grace and dignity to municipal housing'.[29] Building began in 1969, with the very best of intentions, but Hulme was rapidly to become the project which epitomised the very worst of the post-war building boom.

The prefabricated walls and supporting structures of the Crescents were poorly constructed, with bolts and supporting ties missing. The architects designed in a then cutting-edge form of underfloor heating that proved prohibitively expensive after the oil shocks of the 1970s. The balconies on the decks had gaps in them that were perfect for a curious child to sneak through and, after a five-year-old fell to their death, hundreds of Hulme residents signed a petition asking to leave. Eventually, the council responded by limiting the estate to adults only, and then by stopping taking rents altogether. The Crescents became a dangerous place, with decks that the police refused to patrol. There was a certain outlaw romance about all of this. The film critic Mark Kermode once made a radio documentary full of vivid memories of his time living there as a student in the late 1980s, surrounded by Madchester's booming counterculture.[30] It has been described as both an 'adult playground' and 'anarchic in the most pejorative sense of the term', but few regretted the coming of the Barratt homes in 1991.

Britain had been building homes at breakneck speed since the 1950s. The war had devastated the country's housing stock and both main parties wanted to clear the slums that afflicted many inner cities. In the 1940s, Aneurin Bevan had insisted on high-quality housing, even incentivising councils to build in local stone rather than brick. But progress was too slow, and successive governments ratcheted up the subsidies, time frames and political

pressure. Too many places were built quickly and on the cheap.
The boom finally came to an end in the early 1980s, a time
when a third of the population lived in social housing, and that
ending was in no small part thanks to disasters like Hulme. The
Thatcher government slashed subsidies for public housebuilding.
Many of the best council properties were sold under the Right
to Buy and those that were left often decayed to a point where
residents were only too happy to vote for a transfer to a housing
association, which was allowed to borrow money to fund repairs.
The government explicitly decided to shift the way it subsidised
homes: instead of putting money into building, it would subsidise
rents through housing benefits.

The data tells the rest of the story. In the late 1960s Britain
completed well over 300,000 homes a year. By the late 1990s
the number seldom rose above 200,000 and the private sector
contribution flat-lined at around 150,000 until the financial crisis
of 2008 sent completions plummeting across the board.[31] Today
we need nearly a quarter of a million new homes a year to meet
rising demand. In 2012/13, we completed around 107,000.[32]
What essentially happened is that councils stopped building, and
housing associations picked up only a small part of the slack.
Unsurprisingly, the result has been a gigantic boom in house prices
that is slowly rendering parts of the country unaffordable for all but
the wealthiest. The problem is starkest in London. Of the capital's
32 boroughs, only Barking and Dagenham remains affordable, with
homes on the market at just 5.58 times the average salary. This is all
facilitated by Housing Benefit, the costs of which have more than
trebled since the early 1990s. Today, we spend £24bn on Housing
Benefit and £6.5bn on housing development.[33] The government
has put a substantial chunk of public money at the mercy of the
private rental market, being forced to respond to spiralling rents
in order to pay off landlords' buy-to-let mortgages.

Our national failure on affordable housing is, in significant part,
due to the shift from locally run housing policies to what is now a
highly centralised system. Even the housing associations that took
on so much former council housing are oddly centralised creations,
funded and regulated from Whitehall and with no real requirement

for local accountability. Instead of being able to borrow to build homes, councils are forced to negotiate for whatever affordable housing they can get from private developers, with the upper limits of their negotiations effectively capped by the government, and the big house builders always keen to reduce their obligations. Councils and developers occasionally spend substantial sums fighting court cases over how much money a new development will make.

At the same time, the Housing Benefit system gives councils no incentives to build or to get people back into work. This might not matter if Housing Benefit simply rose and fell with the economic cycle, as unemployment benefits tend to. But the truth is that the need for Housing Benefit varies hugely from place to place, depending on the state of the local housing market, the availability of social housing and whether claimants are in work. The only tool available to the Treasury to manage the situation is its ability to make Housing Benefit more or less generous across the whole country. It is a hopelessly blunt instrument. What we really need is to return the powers that councils need to provide more homes in the right places in order to reduce the benefits bill. In some cases, it would actually be cheaper to build a family a new home than to pay their rent in temporary accommodation. One 2011 analysis suggested that by repurposing benefits for building, 10 London boroughs could create 10,000 new affordable housing units and save the exchequer £56 million a year.[34]

Successive governments have tried to cut local councils and local people out of the housing game, leaving them with no incentive to allow building and few powers to coordinate the education facilities, transport links and utilities necessary to make new developments successful. This approach has been driven partly by the failures of places like Hulme, partly by a distrust of local authorities, partly by free market ideology and partly by a very simple desire on the part of national governments to rid themselves of the huge costs of building and maintaining public and social housing. It is an experiment that shows every sign of having failed.

There is no prospect of going back to the huge levels of municipal building seen in the 1960s and 1970s, and the experience of the Crescents and many similar 'streets in the sky' suggests that this is probably for the best. But a small corner of Hulme contains some hints about how local activism might help to solve the problem.

Amid the Barratt homes stand clusters of funkily brutalist flats. They are owned by a housing co-op that grew out of the old Crescents as a sort of 'lifeboat' for the communities that lived there. They might point the way to the future. Across London, councils are starting to build again. The number of units is small for now – Lewisham, for instance, is building just 500 new council homes in the next few years – but it is a lot more than were being built even a few years ago. Enfield has even set up a company and created a £100m line of credit that will allow it to snap up new homes in the borough to solve the housing crisis that was caused by the benefits cap sending hundreds of poorer families out of central London. Ironically, many of the properties they are buying are ex-council flats that they were forced to sell under the Right to Buy. The policy is untested, but the idea of councils setting up municipal companies to buy and build is rapidly gaining support.

Tower Hamlets is also seeing the beginnings of a remarkable experiment. On the site of a former hospital, members of the local community have taken the future of their housing into their own hands. The land under the St Clements site is owned in perpetuity by a foundation set up and owned by the community, and the homes that are currently being built there will have their prices pegged to local incomes. They are likely to cost half the price of homes in neighbouring areas. These new approaches are currently small scale, although we should not forget that one of the ideas that underpin this book is that many micros make a macro. If every council in the country developed community land trusts and bought and built homes, we could magnify the power of an Enfield 150 times over. Giving councils the same powers as their European neighbours to borrow and drive development could start to unlock a new generation of genuinely affordable homes, as long as we learn the lessons of both Hulme and the ineffective national policies that came after.

3 Why we have too many hairdressers and too few builders

Greater Manchester is one of the UK's greatest success stories. The towers of the city centre and the thriving cultural scene are the outward signs of an economy that has blossomed over the 20 years since the mid-1990s. Economists project that the city council and neighbouring Trafford will produce more than 50,000 new jobs between 2014 and 2019, almost as many as Leeds, Edinburgh and Glasgow combined.[35] The city's transport connections, including a municipally owned airport, and its willingness to work with national governments to secure public investment have resulted in the most impressive post-industrial recovery in the country.

But the gleaming buildings conceal a key fact: Greater Manchester has done this without really controlling most of the levers of its own economic destiny. The city's 10 councils have not been able to benefit financially from much of the growth around them because they do not control much of their own tax base. While the city can raise the rate of council tax slightly, it has no control whatsoever over the business rate, which is set and redistributed according to rules set in Whitehall. Stamp duty, income tax and corporation tax all flow back to the Treasury. This means that very little of the growth that has burgeoned around the monolithic Victorian town hall in the city centre has found its way back into local public services or been reinvested in helping the city to grow further. The council has a key role in driving new job creation, and yet it receives just 7% of the benefit of getting someone off benefits and into a living wage job, compared to nearly 80% for the Department of Work and Pensions (DWP) and 10% for the NHS.[36]

The supply of skills in the city is controlled by incentives set in London. Learners can pursue whatever courses they want but often lack good information about what jobs are likely to be available afterwards. Colleges receive a very small amount of their funding based on the long-term employment prospects of the people they teach. The result is a skills mismatch that means that Greater Manchester produces too many hairdressers and not enough people to fill places in its burgeoning creative and media industries. This reflects a national problem: in 2011, 94,000 people completed hair and beauty courses, but there were only 18,000 new jobs in the sector. There is nothing wrong with hairdressing – a good course provides students with generic customer service skills that are useful for lots of jobs – but it is hard to see why we need quite so many hairdressers. Meanwhile the building, engineering and construction sectors were struggling to find qualified employees.[37]

The challenges of managing urban growth have been a recurring theme in British policy. After the war, central governments deliberately tried to disperse the population away from big cities. Green belts were introduced to contain urban sprawl, new towns were created in places like Milton Keynes and Thurrock, and cities like Birmingham were actively discouraged from building new office space in the belief that this would detract from the prospects of struggling northern towns. Local authorities struggled to cope with the wave of deindustrialisation that came to a head along with the financial crises of the 1970s, and the result was a wave of centrally controlled alternatives, ranging from Michael Heseltine's Urban Development Corporations to New Labour's Regional Development Agencies.

But cutting city government out of the picture has neither delivered fairness nor maximised growth. In fact, the economic gap between London and the rest of the country has grown substantially wider over the 30 years since the mid-1980s. As Mike Emmerich, a former director of Greater Manchester's New Economy think-tank, puts it, "There is very strong evidence that the UK's approach to development has been anti-urban and centralising, which has damaged the potential of UK cities to drive economic growth." The needs of Manchester, which faces the big challenges of increasing skills and productivity and reducing worklessness, are different from the needs of Cambridge and Milton Keynes, both of which are set to expand explosively over the coming years. A city like Sunderland is different again, facing as it does the challenge of shifting away from a historical reliance on public sector employment and the need to develop new industries such as offshore wind to secure its economic future.

One-size-fits-all policy simply does not work. The London-centric approach we have had for the past few decades is in some ways even worse, with transport spend in the capital now £2,700 per head, as compared to just £5 in the North-East.[38] It is becoming increasingly clear that reviving our economy requires our politicians to hand more power and money to the hubs of our future growth.

4 Why politicians tinker with structures instead of changing society

In June 2007, Gordon Brown decreed the creation of a new government department. In typical Whitehall fashion, the civil service was given almost no warning. Within days a new permanent secretary and a small team were madly trying to cobble together the Department for Innovation, Universities and Skills (DIUS), which had neither signs nor a website, let alone any staff. At the time, the new organisation seemed like a powerful statement of what would make Mr Brown different from his predecessor: a new economy, based on high-tech industry and a smarter workforce, would set Britain on a course for success in the still-new century. Yet just two years later, the civil servants of DIUS would find themselves clearing their desks, packing up the new signs and turning off the lights. The new economy had lasted a little more than 700 days. Many of DIUS's functions were swallowed up by a gigantic new business department designed to appease the political ambitions of Lord Mandelson.

Centralism provides prime ministers and secretaries of state with an extraordinarily wide range of displacement activities. When you want to signal a change in the political weather, you can simply create a new department. When you want to show that you are modernising a sclerotic public service, you can announce new units and IT programmes. These initiatives very seldom change anything that the public might notice in their daily lives. DIUS is a symbolic case. Whitehall mandarins tend to assume that it takes at least 18 months for a new department to hit its stride. On that basis, DIUS was operating at full capacity for about six months. It cost £14 million to set up and probably more to shut down.[39]

And it was not alone. Between 2005 and 2009 there were more than 90 reorganisations of government departments and quangos, costing the Treasury well over £780 million. Since 1980, 25 new departments have been created, and fewer than half of them still exist. In the United States, the president has created two new departments over the same period.[40] The health service has also been a victim of centralised hyperactivity, undergoing a reorganisation roughly every two years from the mid-1970s to the 2000s.[41] The Labour government's NHS programme for IT is one of the better examples of central hubris, promising a single system for patient care records that would link GPs and hospitals seamlessly. The programme began in 2002 and formally ended nine years later, having delivered little obvious benefit and with its costs overrunning by somewhere between 440% and 770%.[42] By 2011, the Department for Health had localised the whole programme, asking for NHS trusts to develop their own solutions that were compatible with the national infrastructure.

Hubris was not just a disease of the Labour years. It continued under the Coalition government after 2010. Andrew Lansley's massive shake-up of the NHS, for instance, sparked huge resistance from within the health service, forcing an unprecedented 'pause' to reconsider the legislation. It is still too early to judge whether the reforms worked or not, but the view from most observers is 'never again'. Iain Duncan Smith's massive programme of benefits reform has also run into the inevitable problems faced by huge, top-down structural changes, especially those that require sophisticated IT support. Many people think the universal credit is a good idea, combining six benefits into one payment that will provide a sharper incentive for people to get into work. But the original goal of rolling the credit out to one million people by April 2014 was spectacularly missed and the government's Major Projects Authority had to formally 'reset' its progress-chasing with DWP to avoid embarrassing ministers.

These examples are not one-off anecdotes, but the products of our over-centralised system of government. Our electoral system tends to result in stable governments with little need to negotiate or compromise. The weakness of groups like local government, the trade union movement and the professions means that secretaries of state seldom need to negotiate about their plans. Having so much power at the centre means that policy making is often done on an 'all or nothing' basis, with ministers rolling out untested ideas rapidly across the whole country.

Our adversarial style of politics means that it is very hard for governments to admit that they are experimenting, or that some aspects of their policies may not be working. The governing party must always claim that what it is doing is entirely right, and the opposition must claim that it is entirely wrong. In fairness to the politicians, this is what the media, select committees and sometimes even the public demand. This in turn makes it very hard for politicians and civil servants to learn from the past. Whitehall is generally very bad at evaluation, something the mandarins themselves recognise. Releasing a report about the success of your policy is risky business, partly because the opposition will pounce on any evidence of failure and partly because ministers often do not want to be bothered by detailed accounts of policies from a year or two ago, but to move on to the next thing.

All of this leads to hubris, and none of it to good government.

5 Why powerful people feel so powerless

Is it possible to have too much power? Does there come a point where taking on too much power actually starts to make you less powerful, where the outward show of power conceals an inability to really make change happen in society? The answer is obviously 'Yes'. The overmighty Soviet high command governed an economy made up of bogus figures that told it the people were producing heroic quantities of nails and grain, but that were in fact the fabrications of workers and statisticians desperate to please their bosses. The same can be true in warfare, where powerful forces are often either defeated or stymied by smaller and more agile opponents. Simply being able to tell people what to do is no guarantee of being able to deliver the results you want. The extremes of top-down planning were tested to destruction in the 20th century. The UK government no longer controls swathes of major industries, nor seeks to manage the economy to ensure full employment. The rise of transnational bodies like the European Union has constrained national policy makers, while globalisation has weakened their grip on economic development and the flow of people. British politicians have countered these changes by tightening their grip on the domains they can still attempt to control, which are principally those of public services and public behaviour.

Since the 1970s we have seen a startling rise in central government's attempts to secure more power over the wider institutions of the state. Councils have seen a radical reduction in their scope for independent decision making. Governments have given up direct control of services like the NHS, but they have done it as a means to exert more, not less, control over the system. Giving up the pretence that the Department of Health can directly manage the entire NHS and moving to systems of targets and outcome measurement for each hospital is a much more effective way to ensure that the secretary of state gets what they want. Swapping the power to ration hospital care for the power to demand four-hour waiting times while freezing spending is a pretty good deal.

In fact, what we have seen in many policy areas is an attempt by Whitehall to create a direct relationship between central government and the people. Tony Blair once spoke of having 'scars on his back' from standing up to the inefficient public sector on behalf of ordinary working families. As we have seen, the results were attempts to create national policies that cut out the local middle men. Housing policy would consist largely of attempts to create the right incentives for private sector house builders, skills policy would create a market for qualifications, growth policy would involve the all-seeing centre spending money in the regions on behalf of the people of Manchester and Leeds.

The problem is that the markets that were constructed often did not behave very much like real markets at all. In health, patient choice was supposed to restructure the service, scaling down poorer hospitals and increasing finance for the best. But most patients did not exercise their right to choose,[43] preferring their local hospital, and political pressure often kept hospitals open, regardless of their performance. In housing, the political imperatives of the planning system have limited the supply of land and made it more profitable for builders to trade in fields than to build large numbers of homes. The market in volume housebuilding is now dominated by just three big providers who have no real incentive to meet the scale of Britain's housing need, particularly not at the affordable end of the spectrum.[44] There is not a lot of creative destruction going on in these quasi-markets.

The challenge for the politicians is that the only levers they can completely control are those of funding, structures and incentives. These can be extremely powerful and effective, but they cannot tap into the new power that resides in interpersonal relationships. Many of the problems that ministers want to address involve winning hearts and minds, not just setting up frameworks. These problems can be solved only by creating better relationships between different bits of the state, and between the state and the public. New power needs to be governed at a level where interpersonal relationships can be brokered authentically. Sometimes that is the level of the nation-state, but it seems more likely to work at a local level, using platforms that people can genuinely control. This is particularly true when we want to harness new power to allow people to do things in the real world, rather than simply signing petitions. In this context, the best that national policy makers can do is to create a supportive context for collaboration on the ground. The Whitehall world of targets, incentives and flows of money needs to be harnessed to support the local world of convening and collaboration.

Yet, far from being cowed, the central planners are currently emboldened by three new policy-making tools that promise to reinvigorate their ability to create better lives for people. The first is the introduction of design techniques into policy making, with their emphasis on trying to understand services from the citizens' point of view. The second is the development of behavioural economics, which holds the promise that the only thing wrong with the economists' plans for the world is a lack of understanding of individual psychology. Finally, the smart cities movement promises a new panopticon, in which all of our movements around urban areas are anonymously monitored and analysed to make life more seamless. Rio de Janeiro's urban control centre, a room fitted with a gigantic video wall wired to sensors across the city, including 560 cameras, is just the most terrifying example of the phenomenon. It does not help that its mayor, Eduardo Paes, actually describes the centre as being 'like our Big Brother'.[45]

Individually, these developments have the potential to be hugely beneficial for policy makers, and indeed for citizens themselves. They can give us more control over our data, more information about our cities and the ability to put our own behaviour in a wider context socially and ecologically. But the danger is that psychology and technology combine in the hands of anxious civil servants to create a new techno-Fabianism, convincing Whitehall that the only thing that was ever wrong with top-down planning and market making was a lack of good information and behavioural insight. Mike Bracken, the director of the Government Digital Service, suggested on Twitter in February 2015 that technology could remove 'false binaries' between local and central, public and private, user needs and government needs. The truth is that when governments are involved, digital platforms usually serve to obscure the real operation of power. The fact that I can access more government services through a single portal does not necessarily mean that I have any more control over those services. Try telling a disabled benefits claimant facing a computerised assessment for the Personal Independence Payment that there is no binary between their needs and the government's. It is vital that we use the internet to automate transactions between citizen and state, saving money and providing a better user experience. But we need to put technology firmly in its place: online platforms make it possible for peers to collaborate in extraordinary ways, but the central state is not your peer.

As long as it is combined with British centralism, techno-Fabianism is likely to prove a toxic mix; little more than the same old attempt at central control hidden behind a well-designed website. This new panopticon will only add to the congestion, exhaustion and overload of a central government machine that is struggling to understand a complex and constantly shifting world. It will contribute to an approach to government where ministers are using huge amounts of the wrong sort of power in a doomed attempt to drive social change. Unsurprisingly, many of them have become deeply frustrated. You can see it most clearly in the repeated attempts by ministers to blame the Whitehall machine for not delivering on their priorities.

But things are starting to change, and one city more than any other is leading the charge.

THREE

The localist renaissance: how England's cities fought back

For what can be imagined more beautiful than the sight of a
perfectly just city rejoicing in justice alone? (Mark Helprin[1])

In October 2014, nine of Greater Manchester's council leaders
gathered around a table in the city's Victorian Gothic town hall.[2]
Sitting in the midst of this sea of Labour politicians was the
dark form of the Chancellor, George Osborne. He was there to
announce his agreement to plans that would devolve powers over
skills, health and housing to the city under a new, directly elected
mayor. England's second city was set to surpass Boris Johnson's
London, taking on all of the capital's powers along with greater
control over Manchester's further education colleges and welfare
system. Where the capital had been the beneficiary of a benign,
top-down devolution from a sympathetic government, Greater
Manchester's new mayoralty was the product of nearly 30 years of
hard graft. This was a city that had *dragged* power out of the centre.
In doing so, it had broken a decades-long policy consensus. As Mike
Emmerich, a pivotal figure who was then head of the city's New
Economy think-tank, puts it: "In London the weather is usually
pretty good. In Manchester, we have to make our own weather."

The agreement was controversial. It was far from clear that the
people of Greater Manchester wanted a mayor. A similar, but far
more limited, proposal for Manchester City Council had failed
in a referendum just two years earlier. Now it was back on the
table for the whole conurbation, and no one had voted for it. The

Wigan MP, Lisa Nandy, described it as 'a cosy, backroom deal'. Not only that, but the new mayoralty was announced by Osborne on the same day that the Labour leader, Ed Miliband, was in the city, putting forward his own plans for devolution. It looked like Manchester had learned its lesson from the 1980s: don't wait for Labour governments. In fact, the city's councillors were already planning their next move on the path towards regaining their independence from men like Osborne and Miliband. A few months later, in February 2015, it was announced that the city would be taking on responsibility for all of its £6bn health and social care spending. The same deal will soon be offer to other parts of the country as part of George Osborne's 'Northern Powerhouse' initiative.

The level of ambition among the 10 districts that make up Greater Manchester – or 'GM', in the semi-official shorthand of the city's bureaucrats – is breathtaking: to make the conurbation into something approaching a city state. Local public services cost approximately £22.5bn a year; the city generates £17bn a year in taxes. The aim is to close the gap. By reforming public services to cut their cost and increasing productivity across the city, Manchester believes it can pay its own way. That would be the basis of a powerful case for the new mayor and the councils to keep a lot of that money locally and decide how it should be spent. Geoff Little, Deputy Chief Executive at the city council, thinks the conurbation should ultimately have much more power over a whole range of public services:

> "We're absolutely clear that Greater Manchester can take on much more control over the big blocks of public spending. Do we really want to be involved with heart transplants? Absolutely not. But the money that's spent on organising those acute health service activities can be much more effectively organised across a place like GM."

A few months before the elected mayoralty was announced, an independent report[3] called for Greater Manchester to take on five big national property taxes and control of the income tax generated across the conurbation. It had been commissioned by the city fathers, who warmly welcomed its publication. Think about what those recommendations would mean in practice. A conurbation that raised most of its own money and decided how to spend it without needing to ask permission from Whitehall, immune to many of the tools and tricks that the Treasury uses to constrain cities, capable of redesigning health, further education and benefits to meet the needs of local people and not to service the fragmented structures of the civil service machine. If GM can pull it off, it will have kick-started the creation of a very different sort of Britain.

Greater Manchester has won the right to show that a different way of running government is possible, one that is localised, focused on people and communities, and all the more efficient for it. Where it leads, others are already following. How had Greater Manchester cracked the centralist consensus? The trick had involved a large dash of low politics, a certain amount of good fortune and a lot of work. The Chancellor was keen to bolster his party's support in the North, and had already promised a raft of new policies, including a new high-speed railway line connecting Leeds to Merseyside, so as to create a 'Northern Powerhouse'. The near-miss of the Scottish independence referendum the same year had made the government keen to show that it was responding to political disillusionment. At a time when politics was taking a populist turn and money was scarce, the devolution deal offered a cheap way to buy some support. and the new mayoralty opened up the long-term possibility that Greater Manchester could one day be run by a Tory. The current of political ideas was also in favour – a slew of popular books had appeared over the preceding years praising the virtues of pragmatic cities over gridlocked national parliaments in Washington and London.

The conurbation was also lucky. While it was hit hard by deindustrialisation, its location between Leeds and Liverpool, its transport connections across the North, to London and internationally through the municipally owned airport all encouraged the growth of service industries. Merseyside's fissiparous politics in the 1980s and 1990s meant that it had lost investment and talent to its nearby rival.

But the real magic lay in the city's politics. Mancunian municipal socialism had died in 1987 when Margaret Thatcher was elected for her third term and it became clear to even the most optimistic local leaders that the red cavalry would not come riding over the hill with a massive programme of public investment. Starved of funding, the city council's then-leader, Graham Stringer, had nearly joined the left-wing rate-capping rebellion that attempted to defy Thatcher in the mid-1980s, but had been forced to back down by his own moderate backbenchers and the local Conservative opposition.[4] At one time, he had planned a 70-strong economic development team to spend public money in the city.[5] Now, in 1987, he would find himself writing a letter of surrender to the Conservative Environment Secretary, Nicholas Ridley, saying that he was ready to work with the government, which meant working with the private sector. It is not clear that Ridley ever read the letter, but the money nonetheless flowed into the city's urban development corporation and the Hulme city challenge fund that finally demolished the Crescents.

Greater Manchester took an entrepreneurial turn and a new culture of pragmatic partnership working took hold. The goal now was simple: jobs and growth. In a way, it was a return to the flinty pragmatism that had built the Victorian 'Cottonopolis' in the first place. Stringer says today that "Politicians should sit down and think: where should my city be going and what powers have I got, what can I do? I came to that view out of necessity. It was after I went round the world chasing the Olympics and I saw how other cities did it." As the Blair governments turned on the public-spending taps, Manchester was well placed to secure a hefty share for its regionally important education and healthcare facilities. Two attempts to win the Olympics, in 1996 and 2000, had helped Greater Manchester to see itself as a world city, competing against Barcelona, not Birmingham. The 2002 Commonwealth Games only cemented this further. The BBC's decision to relocate a sizeable chunk of its staffing to Salford from 2010 onwards reflected and amplified the city's post-industrial success. When recession struck in 2009, Manchester was better placed than most to recover.

However, the conurbation's greatest stroke of luck was that its 10 councils are too small. Economic activity is focused on the area covered by the city council, but it contains perhaps a fifth of the conurbation's population. Trafford, Tameside and Salford all contain important parts of the city's economy. Large parts of the workforce commute in from places like suburban Stockport and the former mill towns of Wigan and Oldham. No single council can govern an economy that effectively stretches from the edge to the Pennines to the outer fringes of Merseyside. Unlike Birmingham or Leeds, which dominate their regional economies, Manchester City Council had to recognise its interdependence with its neighbours. Creating regional government for the North-West might once have seemed an obvious answer, but that idea was crushed in 2004 when an already reluctant Tony Blair lost a referendum in the North-East. The future of English governance would have to revolve around the city, and that suited Greater Manchester just fine. The question was how to make it happen.

This problem led the city's economists to repurpose a cluster of American ideas called the new economic geography, which essentially held that cities were hotspots for growth because companies working in complementary sectors like to be close to one another. Proximity means that they can share information face to face, leading to more of the chance conversations that generate innovation and new business opportunities. Having a critical mass of companies in a city helps to attract and develop a skilled workforce, while encouraging the development of local support services, supply chains and sub-contractors. This helps to explain why there are so many financial services firms in the City of London and so many biotech firms in Cambridge.

A similar effect has helped to build South Manchester's strengths in areas such as creative, media and sporting industries, but the southern districts could not thrive on their own. They needed investment and people from across Greater Manchester, and if the outlying districts were going to put their money into the south, they needed a say in the process of governing. The whole city needed to work together to invest its money in supporting its growth hotspots and ensuring that the benefits flowed outwards to poorer areas.[6] The result was a unique culture of collaboration that has become increasingly formalised over time. As early as the 1980s, the city's councils already came together regularly to manage the city's airport, a jointly owned asset that had survived the Thatcher era, and during the 1990s they formed partnerships to market their city and bring in new investment. The Association of Greater Manchester Authorities grew to have an important role in coordinating decision making, and the city has had a city-wide 'supercouncil' since 2011, where the leaders of all 10 local authorities come together to take decisions about economic growth.

The clearest results from all of this collaboration can be seen in the massive expansion of the city's metrolink system since the early 1990s. All 10 of the Greater Manchester councils have pooled their transport funding to support the extension of trams across the city, linking people to the growth hotspots in the south. Central government was persuaded to invest in the project on the basis that the new metro connections would boost economic growth and generate a return in the form of income and corporation tax. A share of those national taxes will be returned to the city to recognise the risk it is taking on the scheme. The scheme was managed locally and, unusually for a major transport project, it was delivered before time and on budget. As Jon Lamonte, the chief executive of Transport for Greater Manchester, puts it: "What it reflects is how successful we can be when Greater Manchester is given the funding and power to build something ourselves. It shows the power of what you can do on a local basis."[7]

Of course, Greater Manchester still faces some very severe problems. For all the growth it has managed, it has struggled to connect economic development to social inclusion. The number of people stuck on benefits for the sick and disabled has remained stubbornly high, never falling below 143,000 between 1999 and 2012 and peaking at 172,000. The city's productivity is disappointing for an economy of its size, reflecting an inability to produce enough skilled workers, and transport links that still need improving. Educational attainment remains a significant challenge. The city faces the same spending cuts as everyone else, forcing it to try to meet social problems with less money. The key is to drive forward a series of reforms to work, health and skills that can raise productivity, get people back to work, increase the tax take and start a cycle of growth that will 'lift all boats'.

"This is Manchester, we do things differently here," said Tony Wilson, the founder of Factory Records. Like him, the councils that make up the Greater Manchester experiment combine a certain brilliance with a bucketful of exceptionalism and a lot of swagger. They are convinced that their city is special: a place with a unique ability to grow, with a peculiarly capable leadership, ready to lead the way. The fact that Greater Manchester is blazing a trail for other regional cities is incidental to what the city's leaders really want, which is a more powerful Manchester. It is an attitude that privately annoys the hell out of some of the other big cities. It is certainly true that this experiment is far from perfect. The thing is, it's working.

1 The age of austerity

We live in an age of austerity. There is a cross-party consensus that the country's deficit must be paid down, and that means substantial cuts in public spending. At the same time, demand for healthcare, social care and pension payments is rising as the population ages. On present trends, the costs of services for the elderly will rise from 13% of GDP in 2015 to nearly 19% by the early 2060s,[8] an increase equivalent to the current proportion of GDP spent on the NHS. The result of these pressures is what will probably be at least a decade-long programme of austerity. It will take money away from services that support economic growth and innovation, while protecting hospitals and pensions. There are big questions about whether any government can really stand the course on deficit reduction. The first five years of cuts, from 2010 to 2015, were in part a way to correct the high levels of spending achieved in the Brown years. The next five years of austerity will involve starving already lean public services. Some councils are wondering whether they can keep the streets clean. Even the health service, safe from real-terms cuts, is struggling to keep up with rising demand.

The 2010s are probably not just a lost decade to be followed by another Labour spending splurge, but the beginning of a long-term shift in the role of government in British society. Even if there were not a penny of spending cuts, the state would still face huge pressure to change. Governing institutions evolve in tandem with the economy and society around them – look at the rise of the municipal corporations to run burgeoning Victorian cities – and we are currently living at the start of an economic transformation that is being driven by networked computing and automation. The tech-utopians and libertarians are likely to be disappointed: governments show no sign of turning into smart customer-service platforms, nor of becoming residual and irrelevant. But technology is about to revolutionise our economy, and this will have huge implications for politics and power.

The tremors of the coming earthquake have been felt in the music business and the book industry, by taxi drivers and journalists, but in the coming years many more of us will feel the earth shifting under our careers. One recent study showed that almost half the US workforce could be replaced by computers and robots over the coming decades.[9] Some kinds of work will simply disappear – from data-entry clerks to anything that involves driving, probably including whole mining operations. New jobs and a new economy will emerge. The first wave of post-war automation combined with globalisation to spur the deindustrialisation of Britain's regional cities. If that wave of economic change led to the centralism of the Thatcher era, the second wave of data-driven automation of white-collar jobs looks set to do the opposite, by opening up the possibility of a decentralised economy of creative cottage industries.

The decentralisation of everything from film-making to manufacturing means people can produce goods and services from their own homes that would have been unimaginable even a decade ago. The rise of increasingly efficient sources of renewable power means that energy is likely to become a lot cheaper; the widespread use of rooftop solar panels meant that, on a sunny day in 2014, coal-power generators in Queensland, Australia actually started paying people to take their excess energy. In March 2015, Costa Rica went for 75 days using only renewables, thanks to the country's smart use of hydroelectric generation and heavy rainfall. If efficient networks of renewable energy can be linked to driverless transportation, clever machines and sensors and smarter manufacturing techniques such as 3D printing, then technology could radically reduce the marginal cost of producing a physical item in the same way that it has already reduced the cost of reproducing a book or a music album.[10] We could easily design and produce everything from furniture to tools at low cost in or near our homes. Many techno-optimists believe this development might usher in a world of abundance that would replace capitalism itself with a new mode of production based on collaborative commons (see Chapter Four). At the very least, these developments will make it easier for decentralised networks of smaller businesses to compete with the big boys.

We are not quite heading for the medievalist paradise that William Morris had in mind, but technology is making his ideal of self-governing craftsmanship look a bit less utopian. Arguably, the process has already begun. On some measures, a cluster of creative and technology industries, known as the 'flat white economy' after the favourite coffee of East London hipsters, is already contributing 7.6% of the UK's GDP,[11] and that figure could double by 2025. Much of this activity is clustered in London and associated with such horrors as cafes serving designer porridge at £5 a bowl. The challenge may be to turn the flat white economy of beardy techies into a far more inclusive William Morris economy of mass craftsmanship that makes sense to joiners in Manchester and carpenters in Liverpool as well as the user-experience designers in the East End of the capital. Of course, new technology is also making some pretty dystopian futures possible: what happens when the wealthy can use technology to casualise or completely replace their workforces? Can the new economy create jobs fast enough to replace those it is killing off? If not, then how will we cope with the resulting unemployment? The biggest question of the 21st century may be whether we create a world that is closer to Morris's fantasies of human potential unleashed, where work becomes more like play, or Charles Dickens' tales of that same potential squandered by social injustice and deadened imaginations.

We do not know what government will do in the economy to come, but it seems clear that part of the answer is 'less'. One tantalising glimpse of the future is offered by Casserole Club, an app being tested by councils that encourages people to cook an extra plate of food and take it to an elderly neighbour, reducing social isolation and saving on social care costs. Another is offered by the growth of wearable wristbands that monitor people's health, theoretically allowing us to upload our vital signs every day to the NHS, where they can be automatically analysed for early signs of asthma or heart conditions. All of this suggests that we have probably passed the maximum size and influence of the public sector for the foreseeable future, partly because we cannot afford as much government but mostly because we might not need as much of it any more. If we can do more for ourselves, if we can connect to each other easily, if we can govern at least partially without government, then Westminster becomes a lot less important and much less relevant.

For now, Britain's politicians have no clear answers about how the cuts are going to be managed. For the Conservatives, not having a plan is almost a point of principle. Their idea is that something better will emerge through a Schumpeterian process of creative destruction. Cutting the state is in itself the answer to what the future of government should look like. Labour's response is to try to preserve as far as is possible the existing range and quality of public services. Both major political parties maintain that everything will be fine: we can reduce the size of the state and keep taxes down while simultaneously keeping public services much as they are. Local authorities that face 40% cuts over the current decade are told that sharing their back offices and senior officials will solve the problem, when the evidence clearly shows that the savings are relatively small. The only answer politicians seem able to offer for the NHS is ever more money. It looks very much as if national politicians have quit the field and are hoping someone else will sort it out. Increasingly, it looks as if that someone will be a city like Greater Manchester.

There are two possible responses to a situation like this. One reading suggests that the current financial climate is the final stage of a very long process of ending the local role in British politics. In this reading, George Osborne's plans for devolution are simply a way to devolve the public spending axe to an ever-weaker set of local institutions. Another says that when central politicians have no answers, it is time for local places to start providing them. Greater Manchester suggests that the latter view is winning the argument. The plans currently emerging from England's cities represent nothing less than an attempt to reform the state from the ground up, fixing the broken systems bequeathed by the centre.

The future of the local is no longer just about councils. As Greater Manchester is demonstrating, it is about creating new relationships between different parts of the public sector, and between the public sector and the people it serves. Where national policy makers find their formal policy levers increasingly ineffectual, cities are finding their ability to convene and persuade far more powerful. Their task over the next five years is to show how increased decentralisation can help to rebuild public services from the ground up by integrating fragmented local provision, restoring the link between economic growth and social progress and finding better ways to manage the rising tide of demand for public services.

2 Breaking down bureaucracy

In 2012, a despairing Thomas Friedman returned from the Republican Party convention in the US. Mitt Romney had been chosen as the party's candidate for President, but in all the speeches and announcements there had been no great journey to symbolise American hope and ambition. Where was the equivalent of John F. Kennedy's promise to go the moon, asked the *New York Times* columnist, and what public policy challenge could possibly justify such a grand promise today? Friedman's answer: keeping the nation's kids in school.[12] Half of young Americans were not properly prepared for kindergarten, and the consequences reverberated all through the education system in the form of under-attainment and high drop-out rates. The next day came a letter from Nancy Zimpher, a former president of the University of Cincinnati in Ohio: 'We need a map, as Mr Friedman suggests, and we've got one.'[13]

In 2006, Ohio was a microcosm of the United States' huge problems with public education. Local students were simply not performing well enough and the state ranked 42nd in the US in terms of the attainment of bachelor's degrees among its youth. Cincinnati did not lack for public and voluntary activity designed to support young people. What it lacked was coordination. Lots of effort from individual organisations all working separately was not adding up to decent results. Cincinnati's education system was programme rich, but system poor. Zimpher became a key part of the solution: a new partnership called Strive. The idea was to bring together a huge range of public, private and voluntary organisations to focus on improving educational attainment. A small, core organisation coordinated research and development and forged a consensus across the city around five goals, and a route map for achieving them, setting out the interventions that kids needed at each step of their development in order to succeed. Everyone was expected to buy into the map; it took three years.

The whole partnership is supported by huge amounts of research and data analysis to understand what works, which has now been formalised into a single dashboard where each pupil's record is constantly updated by all the different partners working with them. The learning is shared with local schools and charitable foundations to help them target their grant money. Local businesses are involved in providing consultancy support and advice to help not-for-profits run successful businesses, as well as contributing some funding. The programme's success has led to the creation of a national organisation called StriveTogether, which by the spring of 2015 had helped over 60 communities in the US to set up similar initiatives.

We tend to assume that public services are designed and organised to help the public, but they are more usually a compromise between the needs of ordinary people and the demands of powerful professional groups. Doctors, teachers and underground drivers all have a say in the way their services are managed, but the most powerful profession of all is the civil service. Whitehall is structured into a series of departmental baronies, each with a huge amount of autonomy. This means that they are more concerned with administering the health service, or the benefits system, than with handling big problems that cut across departments. That is probably fine most of the time. It seems likely that about 80% of the work of government can be organised fairly well through command-and-control hierarchies, but that means 20% cannot, and the problems that fall into that one-fifth of state activity are often the most difficult and expensive. It means that British government is very bad at helping people with multiple needs – the troubled family beset by poor parenting, benefit dependency and crime, or those poverty-stricken older people with diabetes and a heart condition who are struggling to afford the rent.

As we have seen, the Department of Health is overwhelmingly concerned with managing the NHS budget, and the costs of hospital care tend to be at the very top of its agenda. Almost all of its money gets spent on treatment. Local government can help to stop people needing to go to hospital in the first place, but the two services struggle to work together effectively, partly because they operate under very different systems of centrally-set targets and incentives. The same is true in welfare, where councils can help to get people back into work, but receive very little reward for doing so. Vertical management from Whitehall trumps horizontal management in towns and cities. Leaving aside the human costs of getting the wrong treatment, or failing to find a job, some estimates suggest that the failure of different parts of the public sector to work together costs as much as £4bn a year.[14] This is a hugely wasteful way to run a government.

Strive embodies a completely different logic, and it works: in Cincinnati, after nine years, 91% of the indicators for pupil success were moving in the right direction. There was a 13% jump in kindergarten readiness. Fourth-grade reading achievement for Cincinnati Public School students was up 21%. High school graduation and college completion was also up. The StrivePartnership in Cincinnati has succeeded because it seeks to mobilise the collective resources of a place around a shared problem. Rather than maximising the effectiveness of schools, it is trying to maximise the effectiveness of everyone involved in raising educational attainment through the way it targets money and the way it shares knowledge. The key to success is having a shared agenda, a shared measurement system and constant communication to provide feedback to all the participants. It is an approach we might call government by learning, and it can thrive only at the local level.[15]

The Strive approach does not travel straightforwardly into the British context: we have a larger state and do not need the levels of philanthropy and not-for-profit activity that occur in some US cities. But the concept of collective impact – the idea that we need lots of organisations all pulling in the same direction – is putting down roots in England's cities.

In Salford, just to the west of Manchester city centre, the council and local healthcare providers are embarking on an experiment. One of the biggest challenges facing them is an ageing population, with more people developing long-term conditions like diabetes. Too many older people end up in A&E when they could be treated at home or by a GP. Once they are in the hospital system, they can easily get stuck there. They may be well enough to leave hospital, but not well enough to go home alone, in which case they need a place in a properly equipped care home, or a social worker to keep an eye on them. The problem is that the social care services are provided by local government, not by the health services. Salford's solution is an alliance contract.

A normal contract is an agreement between two people. Salford's is an agreement between one buyer – the hospital – and an alliance made up of the council, the clinical commissioning group, the hospital, local hospice and mental health services. They all sign up to deliver the same goals, forcing everyone to work together and support each other, because if one partner doesn't deliver, no one else can either. The council and the health service have pooled their money to create a single shared budget worth £98 million. If it doesn't work, they both lose. The approach is now being scaled up to work across Greater Manchester as the city prepares to take on new responsibilities for all health and social care spending.

Greenwich already provides a small example of what the future relationship between health and local government could look like. If you go to the A&E department at the Queen Elizabeth hospital in Woolwich, you will be assessed to see if you could be treated by a GP or a social worker instead of being admitted to an expensive hospital bed. This means that more people are treated close to home and end up either in a hospice or back home in their own bed much faster. Teams of social workers patrol the wards to make sure that they quickly identify people who are well enough to leave hospital and get them into an intermediate care bed as quickly as possible. Very few of us really want to spend an extra night in hospital, and getting us safely out is better and cheaper all round.

Over time, this approach could develop into a model where councils and hospitals go into business together, setting up dedicated micro-hospitals, or perhaps 'supersurgeries' in the community to provide low-level treatment and help people to manage long-term conditions like diabetes. The idea has been pioneered in the US by ChenMed, a company that has redesigned the GP surgery to stop patients needing to go to hospital. The company hires adapted vans to bring people to its clinics – lack of transport is a key reason why elderly people do not seek attention, makes checking-in easy with a swipe card, has automated administration procedures to allow doctors to focus on patients and on-site pharmacies to ensure that people receive and take their prescriptions. The organisation's patients spend 40% less time in hospital than the national average.[16]

The idea that different parts of the public sector should work together to solve public problems seems so obvious, but Britain's centralised approach to government makes it far harder than it should be for local leaders to bring the fragmented parts of the system back together. Now, local people are starting to put back together what Westminster has put asunder.

3 How cities are creating inclusive growth

In 2011, the governor of Maryland announced the state's biggest-ever round of venture capital funding. Martin O'Malley planned to auction tax credits to insurance companies to raise £100 million.

With the state's privately owned venture capital sector flagging in the wake of the banking crisis, the government decided to step in. O'Malley planned to buy a stake in some of country's hottest start-ups and, in doing so, to attract them to his state. If he earned a little money for the state in return, then so be it. When the results of the venture capital round were announced in 2014, it turned out that O'Malley had bagged companies from West Virginia and Washington.[17]

State venture capital is not a new idea in the US – about 35 of the states have such a fund – but O'Malley wanted to do things on a bigger scale. He had learned from bitter past experience with economic development policy. In the late 1990s, Maryland had offered the Marriott hotel chain a $44m retention subsidy to stay in the state, after it had already decided not to relocate.[18] A study in Connecticut showed that government subsidises to business usually became a very expensive way to create quite a small number of jobs. Maryland combined equity investment with a network of state-supported business incubators, providing cheap office space and advice to start-ups: it has been hailed by the US Chamber of Commerce as the best state for entrepreneurship.

The idea that cities should take a stake in growing local businesses sounds very strange to British ears, the sort of thing that the Thatcher revolution should probably have confined to history. In fact, councils are already taking on a new lease of entrepreneurial life. Manchester owns an airport, Birmingham owns a shopping centre – the Pallasades – which it bought as it was assembling the land that it needed to redevelop the previously shabby New Street Station. The council has revitalised what is now known as Grand Central and is now selling it to help settle a £1bn equal pay claim. Perhaps most extraordinarily, tiny Woking District Council built a renewable energy business that has reduced the council's emissions by 70%, has assets worth £25 million and is providing energy in nearby Milton Keynes.[19]

This kind of entrepreneurship is likely only to grow in importance. One of the biggest challenges Britain faces from 2015 to 2020 is to ensure that a rising economic tide lifts all boats. This means connecting the poor and unskilled to jobs, ensuring that those jobs pay a good-enough wage so that employees can get off state benefits and improving productivity to generate more wealth, making people more independent and providing more funding for local public services. The private sector seems unlikely to do this on its own. Between 2003 and 2007 the economy grew by 11%, but median incomes stagnated.[20]

For a city like Greater Manchester this is a serious problem. Local universities produce a steady supply of ready-made workers, a significant number of whom settle there after graduation, but their efforts are diluted by the very high levels of young people leaving school with few or no useful qualifications. Greater Manchester's councils face a complex set of challenges that can be resolved only locally. The city needs to work with local skills providers and schools to improve educational attainment. This means finding a way to introduce more strategic planning into the fragmented system of apprenticeships, further education colleges and private provision to ensure that they churn out fewer hairdressers and more construction workers. The planners need to build more houses in the parts of Greater Manchester where skilled workers want to live – typically the south of the city and the affluent Cheshire commuter belt. Perhaps most difficult of all, Greater Manchester's councils have to find a way to increase the demand of local businesses for higher skills – there is no point churning out computer scientists if local companies cannot put them to work – and to create career paths that allow people with no skills to work their way up to a decent wage.

Many of the policies that are currently driving growth in Britain's cities were shaped by recession. In essence, central government passes funds to Local Enterprise Partnerships or combined authorities to spend on transport links and capital projects that are designed to increase the pace of economic development. But as the economy returns to growth, these policies will start to look outdated. Private sector investment will start to flow again and public spending will become less important. In this new world, cities need a radically new approach to economic growth that seeks to encourage the future sources of prosperity for their cities and to make sure that the poorest can share in that prosperity.

In the north of Manchester, hard up against the Pennines, the metropolitan district of Oldham has become a shopkeeper. The council's leader, Jim McMahon, was concerned about the number of local people who were being forced to take on expensive credit deals from payday lenders or loan sharks in order to buy basics like furniture and white goods. All the market had to offer the people of Oldham was expensive debt. The town invested its money in a new high street shop in the Spindles shopping centre where staff were judged less on the value of the sales they were making and more on the amount of money they were saving for local people.[21]

McMahon's council is also at the forefront of a wider movement to improve the lives of poorer people across the country. The council pays staff the living wage, an hourly rate set slightly higher than the minimum wage and calculated to ensure that the recipient can afford the basics of a decent life-style. Forcing companies to pay above the minimum wage nationally is a non-starter, because not every business can afford to pay an enhanced rate immediately without destroying jobs. Local government is well placed to know where to exert pressure, provide help and twist arms. Oldham's latest plan is a jobs guarantee for young people, using donations from local businesses to support school leavers to set up their own businesses.

Peterborough is doing things on a grander scale in the energy market.[22] There is a widespread consensus that UK power generation is not working effectively, with an uncompetitive market dominated by six huge, vertically integrated suppliers, and consumers often reluctant to switch suppliers. The result during the economic downturn of the early 2010s was sharply rising energy bills. Peterborough decided to intervene, setting up an energy company to generate solar power. Schools and council buildings were covered with PV panels, reducing the council's costs. This, combined with further development of renewables and the council's energy from waste plant, should enable Peterborough to become a net exporter of green power, partnering with the private sector to put energy into the grid. The aim is to generate both social value for residents and a financial return to the council, helping Peterborough to support its public services by going into business.

In Birmingham, the council is using its own spending with the private sector to try to shift the behaviour of local businesses. The Birmingham Business Charter for Social Responsibility requires anyone who receives a contract from the council to sign up to employing local people, paying the living wage and providing broader social value to the city. This is a big deal: Birmingham spends about £1bn a year, and it wants 30% of that to go to firms that sign up to the charter and produce an action plan for making that commitment a reality, particularly in the more deprived parts of the city. As one cabinet member says: "We knew that every extra pound earned by people in Birmingham would be spent on industry and commerce within Birmingham – creating a virtuous circle to try and solve chronic unemployment and low wages associated with large parts of Birmingham."[23]

Back in Ohio, Martin O'Malley's decision to turn his state into an investment vehicle points the way to a new synthesis of municipal socialism with red-blooded capitalism, one in which councils use their money to encourage social justice through commercial means. It is a powerful idea that a new generation of British Joseph Chamberlains are starting to grasp enthusiastically.

4 Why understanding personal behaviour can save public services

The debate about local public services tends to focus on budget cuts, but growing demand is at least as large a problem. The ageing population is putting pressure on a whole range of care services, rising numbers of A&E attenders are pressuring the NHS and a rising population is having children at a faster rate than local schools and childcarers can handle. Local leaders have only two choices in this situation. They can either ration their services, forcing people at the back of the queue to wait, or they can try to find clever new approaches that meet public need in cheaper and better ways. In 2010, Coventry started to do just that. Like many others, the council was struggling to cope with the costs of transporting children with special educational needs to school. Medical advances mean that people with learning disabilities can live longer, fuller lives than ever before. Like our longer life spans, this is fundamentally a cause for celebration. But it is a fact to which many of our public service have been slow to adapt. Coventry faced a 20% overspend and a group of parents with justifiably high expectations of the service the council would provide.

The city found the solution in the emerging world of behavioural economics. Rather than just cut the service or impose a new approach on its residents, Coventry held a series of focus groups where it identified three distinct attitudes to change among parents. A fairly wealthy group were named the pioneers, interested in independence and embracing new ideas. A second group were labelled the prospectors, people who were seeking wealth and status. A third group, the settlers, were traditional, conservative and risk averse.

Coventry decided that it wanted to shift from a transport service provided by the council to one where parents were given their own budget and training to get their children to school, with the idea being that parents could share taxis or take turns to drive each other's children, thereby saving money. What the focus groups told the council was that it needed to start with the pioneers: they were encouraged to see the personal budgets as a way to take control of their children's lives. As they took up the personal budgets, the prospectors would start to see the new approach as a status symbol, eventually making it seem normal to the settlers. The project saved upwards of 15% of the council's budget in its first year.[24]

Technology is enabling other councils to take even more radical approaches. Newcastle City Council, for instance, is currently developing a mobile phone app that will help young people with special educational needs to use public transport independently. The app will draw on a smartphone's map function, showing the user which bus stop to use, which number bus to take and alerting them to when they need to get off. It could even show them a picture of the right coins to use to pay the driver. All of this could be tracked by parents. The applications of Coventry's behavioural insight work are obvious here.

Perhaps most radically of all, Northamptonshire County Council is using the internet to completely reframe the way people access elderly care. At the moment, most councils bulk-purchase large numbers of care places from a relatively small number of big providers. The council's social care director has to act as the voice of everyone who needs help. The county council's plan is to follow a number of other authorities in moving radically away from this model. Their plan is to give a personal budget to everyone who needs elderly care, much like the ones Coventry introduced for school transport, and to ask them to spend it on a website called Breeze-e. The council's role will no longer be to negotiate a handful of gigantic contracts, but to help people to buy their own care and to ensure there is a thriving market of local personal carers and care homes to support this change. Northamptonshire will no longer be able to use its monopoly buying power to keep prices down, but the fact that local people will be able to choose the service they want, and change it easily if they do not like it, will provide an alternative form of competitive pressure. The site will even provide a small financial return to the council, which gets a cut of the transaction costs.

This, then, is the future of local public services. More websites, fewer people. Less having it done for you and more getting support to do it for yourself. In 2012, a study suggested that maximising the returns from this sort of approach could save as much as £2.5bn in local government alone.[25] That probably overstates matters, but, even if it were worth just half that amount, demand management is part of the answer to maintaining quality while cutting costs.

5 Towards the new British city states

By now, you should be able to see the outlines of a new, more localised world starting to emerge from the fog of the future. It is a world in which cities play a much bigger role in the government of Britain, where local organisations work together seamlessly to make sure that a rising economic tide really does lift all boats and where technologically-enhanced public services give us more choice over our own destiny. It is a world in which local leaders are a bit less concerned with emptying the bins and a lot more interested in the role they can play in creating the conditions for

human flourishing, taking on more of the responsibility for creating
a context in which good lives are possible. While, on the one hand,
our economy seems to be becoming ever more globalised, on
the other, the growth of clusters of high-productivity industries
means that it has never been more localised. The key relationship
is increasingly between the city and the world, and this means that
the city increasingly becomes the place where we have to struggle
for social justice. As the urbanist Richard Florida argues:

> In this new stage of capitalism – call it the knowledge
> economy, the postindustrial economy, whatever – place
> itself has become the key social and economic organizing
> unit: where the knowledge workers congregate, where the
> infrastructure of capitalism is built … And [with] this packing
> in of people … it is place itself that supplants, becomes the
> social and economic organizing unit of modern capitalism,
> analogous to the factory.[26]

The vision of a new sort of city state remains fragile. Devolution
can only really work within a benign national policy environment
– the UK's unbalanced post-industrial economy means that
Merseyside and Manchester still need money from London and
the South East to invest in their economies and meet social need,
at least for the foreseeable future. Without that, localism is just the
freedom for some places to be poor. Localism also represents a
threat to vested national interests: more power for Manchester is
less for ministers and civil servants. Nervous civil servants could
still snuff out the new city-states tomorrow. Budget cuts might
spur astonishing innovation in some places, but create despair and
despondency in others.

But the biggest challenge for localism is that the charge is being
led by councils, not people. And councils have spent the last 20
years getting better at playing Whitehall at its own game: this debate
has become a technocrat-on-technocrat wrestling match. Anyone
with even a passing experience of local politics will know that
there is no inherent reason why local government should be any
less authoritarian than Whitehall. There are inspirational urban

leaders, for sure, but there are also figures that resemble *Spin City*'s bungling mayor Randall Winston or Kelsey Grammar's thuggish Tom Kane. For the new city-states to flourish, we have to bring citizens back into the heart of the discussion.

If there is a critique of what Greater Manchester is starting to achieve, it is the one we heard earlier from the Wigan MP, Lisa Nandy, about cosy backroom deals. If devolution is all about putting power into the hands of ordinary citizens, then why was the decision to create the mayor taken by 10 council leaders with no real input from the people of the city? The truth is that Manchester's devolution is a preoccupation of the city's political elite, and that the extraordinary coherence and confidence of that elite is both an enormous strength and a weakness. The work they have done to revitalise their city is extraordinary, but so is the fact that the political correspondent of the *Manchester Evening News* described local reaction to the mayoral deal as 'apathy'. The word people from outside the city – and even a few insiders – use most consistently about Greater Manchester's leadership is 'mafia', a pointed term that suggests admiration mingled with a touch of suspicion. This is a city whose political leaders and council officers are generally home grown, building up a culture of trust and collaboration over years, if not decades. It is a place where success for a young council official often requires you to 'dip your hands in the blood'.

No amount of public service reform can remove the fact that councils, colleges and hospitals do not have enough money to meet social need. Many parts of the country are grappling with new ways to fund basic services like parks, theatres and even street cleaning. The answer in most cases is that the council will have to pull back and persuade the public to contribute more in terms of either money, time or changed behaviour. If you are not prepared to pick up the litter in your local park, you might have to accept that it will be a mess. If you are not prepared to pay a bit more for a swim at your local leisure centre, you may soon have to start using the private gym over the road.

The only way we can maintain anything like the current quality and scope of public services is to persuade ordinary people to change their behaviour and do more to help themselves and each other. You cannot do that with a citywide plan for economic growth or a programme of alliance contracting, no matter how good it is. Just as importantly, a decentralised Britain will be sustainable only if it puts down deep roots in the fertile soil of civil society. We tend to see our neighbourhoods as places that we pay someone else to look after. The key to a more decentralised society is to change that attitude. A neighbourhood is actually a common: a thing we all benefit from, but which none of us really owns. That means we all have a duty to look after it. As we push power down to the local level, we need the people living there to reach out and grab it. That is exactly what is starting to happen.

FOUR

From consumers to creators: reinventing citizenship from the ground up

> What we always meant by socialism wasn't something you forced on people, it was people organising themselves as they pleased into co-ops, collectives, communes, unions ... if socialism really is better, more efficient than capitalism, then it can bloody well compete with capitalism. So we decided, forget all the statist shit and the violence: the best place for socialism is the closest to a free market you can get. (Ken McLeod[1])

Birmingham's central library is an architectural masterpiece, a temple to learning rising over the city centre, an emblem of its regeneration. The only problem is that the people of the city will not be able to spend all that much time in it. In 2015, budget cuts forced the council to announce that it would almost halve the opening hours. Perhaps the people of Birmingham should feel lucky to still have their library at all. Across the country, some 200 closed in 2012 alone,[2] driven by the twin pressures of cuts and falling visitor numbers, which at one point pushed the cost of issuing a book in a few areas to over £8 a pop.[3] That would be just about enough to buy each borrower a paperback of their choice whenever they wanted it. There is perhaps no other part of the public sector quite so ripe for technological transformation as the internet puts e-books within easy reach of anyone with a computer. Is this the end for buildings full of books? Some community activists have a very different idea about what a library might be like, and in an unloved corner of Essex they have started to build it.

Annemarie Naylor specialises in helping communities to take things over.[4] One of her recent projects involved designing a resident-led broadband scheme to bring affordable WiFi to a deprived estate in Merthyr Tydfil. As the cuts started to bite in 2010, she found herself advising and networking among more than 65 communities that were trying to save their local libraries. Naylor specialises in finding new business models – identifying the often well-hidden sources of money, energy and effort that can keep an asset like a pub or community centre alive. But with libraries she faced a challenge. These were often small buildings in deprived or rural areas. They had little space available to rent out or turn into cafes.

Libraries are a tough service to commercialise: the whole point is that books and information should be free at the point of use. For all the innovation that was taking place around children's activity classes and internet access, there was nothing that could obviously provide the revenue to make a library independent. Indeed, many of the most innovative international ideas involve the wholesale digitisation of library services – some even envisage railway station walls being painted with an image of library shelves, each book being denoted by a QR code that can be scanned and downloaded there and then.

But what if the whole point of a library were different? Naylor had watched community activists in Burnley trying to bring an old library back into use, using games consoles and benches covered in electronic components to encourage local people to play and to tinker. Rather than a space where people went to consume things, could a library become a place where they went to *make* things? Might it be a place for learning and doing together, not just for reading alone?

The opportunity came early in 2012, when Naylor became involved in a project to bring an old bus-station waiting room in Colchester back into use. As well as a reasonably large indoor space, there were two outward-facing kiosks standing unused on the site. The whole thing was awaiting demolition, but the plans to regenerate the area had stalled with the banking crisis. A group of volunteers helped to revitalise the waiting room and open up the space as an incubator for local small businesses that rented space, thus helping to provide some much-needed money for the project. But the heart of the waiting room became what Naylor calls a 'hack-maker space', with a tool library and regular classes on how to design and build artefacts.

The chief currency of the new library is the maker kit, for which members provide the instructions and materials that you need to make a project. On one of the Waiting Room's regular Maker Wednesdays a local entrepreneur showed library users how to make a simple games console using a basic Raspberry Pi microprocessor. The project now sits in boxes, waiting to be checked out by people who want to try it at home; there is a small charge for the components, but the assembly instructions can be borrowed for free. The Waiting Room doesn't just help people to learn and make, it is also a repository for their projects. If you make something there, you leave behind a copy (and the instructions for others to make it). The only people who are charged are those who use the space to make something overtly commercial.

"This is about moving from libraries as a platform for reading or accessing information to one which is read/write, like the internet," says Naylor. "We want to reflect the digital developments of the past 15–20 years and, with that, the vast amount of cultural data – people's thoughts, knowledge and know-how – that are published by us all everyday online but, for some reason, are not swelling our traditional memory institutions."

The Waiting Room is a prototype designed to prove that the concept of the library can evolve so that it becomes a place where people make things as well as consume information. Set up outside the traditional structures of local government, the Waiting Room is an attempt to show that self-governing local institutions can play a key role in meeting social needs in the 21st century. The idea is spreading. Naylor is now working with 35 areas of the country to bring her concept into the state system, and maker materials from the Waiting Room have travelled around the country to fuel science and technology events. The idea is that Waiting Room-

style 'Common Libraries' will initially fit in alongside traditional
public libraries. The aim is not to supplant buildings and books,
although there is clearly a possibility that 'hack-maker spaces' will
one day rewrite the Victorian source code of one of our oldest
public institutions.

1 Beyond markets and states

The Waiting Room is just one example of a burgeoning realm of
do-it-yourself social action that is taking place beyond the market
and the state. Lots of people have different names that try to
capture all of this activity. You might like to call it the social sector,
the third sector or the civic economy. But each of these makes
it sound as if the realm of social activity is basically just another
form of the public or private sectors, highly structured by power
or money. In fact, what makes this kind of social action inspiring
is the way that it accesses resources that the other sectors cannot
touch: the voluntary resources of community, gifting and shared
endeavour without direct financial reward. The Waiting Room
does need money in order to function, but that isn't why it really
works. It draws on resources that we can create only when we
come together and create together. We all use these resources to
get through our daily lives, but none of us owns them. They form
a huge part of our economy – on some measures, unpaid work is
the equivalent of 77% of GDP[5] – they are what many people now
call *the commons*. Yet we pay worryingly little attention to growing
and nurturing them.

One day in the late 1960s, the economist Elinor Ostrom went
to a lecture at Indiana University. The speaker was Garrett Hardin
and his topic was the tragedy of the commons.[6] Hardin argued
that the problem with unregulated resources was that people had
every incentive to consume them and no one had any power to
stop them doing so. Take a piece of common land in an agricultural
community. Every herdsman has an incentive to graze as many
of his animals as possible for free, but if they all do so, then the
common will rapidly become barren. The common resource will
be destroyed. It is not hard to find examples where Hardin was

right: the communities of the north-eastern American coast, for instance, are still suffering from generations of overfishing of cod stocks. The answer, according to Hardin, was to recognise that commons did not work. Ensuring that resources were owned and regulated by either business or government was the best way to maintain them.

Ostrom smelled a rat. Her work since the 1950s had started to show that Hardin was not always right. In fact, she came to see him as a totalitarian, a man who blamed the welfare state for encouraging overbreeding and creating the conditions for a Malthusian catastrophe. Ostrom argued that examples of the tragedy of the commons were not as widespread as Hardin had suggested and that they were often fairly easy to solve.[7] Traditional societies had spent centuries developing complex systems of rules to govern the watercourses and common land upon which their lives depended. In England and Wales, use of the common land was restricted to 'commoners', and there were limits on the number of people who could use overgrazed land. Medieval peasants may have been many things, but they were not stupid. Ostrom's studies showed that the apparently messy structure of Californian water governance or US urban policing often resulted in surprisingly efficient and effective outcomes. Her work on what she called 'common pool resources' eventually earned her the Nobel prize for economics.

The internet turbocharges the idea of the commons because it creates a platform upon which millions of people can cooperate to make things. Wikipedia is a totemic example of what some have called commons-based peer production, a new form of production which brings together huge numbers of people to produce shared information goods ranging from software to online encyclopedias. Wikipedia is an example of what is sometimes called the 'knowledge commons', a world of shared information that people can access anywhere, anytime and that is best organised on a globally open basis so that as many people as possible can participate. Even though the internet cannot provide the answer to a real-world problem like the decline of libraries, it does provide a powerful set of metaphors and ideas to inspire the tangible, commons-based projects of people like Annemarie Naylor. From Wikipedia to water management, the lesson is that, contra Hardin, people actually can be trusted to organise themselves in many circumstances, and they often do it more effectively than formal bureaucratic institutions.

This is a lesson that developed countries like the United Kingdom are having to relearn. After a very long period of growth in the size of government, we have become used to the idea that there are certain things the state should do, both practically and morally. The idea that it might be better if people were helped to do more for themselves sounds dangerously like a return to the 1930s. But whether you approve of the idea or not, you cannot afford to ignore it. As Dan Corry, the former head of Gordon Brown's policy unit and now chief executive of a voluntary sector think-tank, says: "In practice the community – whatever that means – has got to be much more important in providing services in different ways and councils have got to think about how they do that and central government has to think about how it can help enable them to do that better."

A wide range of factors are pushing ideas about self-help and mutual aid firmly back onto the social agenda. One factor is, quite simply, high levels of distrust in government and the business community. Remember that over two-thirds of us trust neither big business nor big government in the wake of the financial crisis that these two sectors created together. If we trust neither the state nor the market, then we need to find something else that we can put our trust in. Another factor is the massive expansion of higher education, the growth of the creative industries and cheap technological tools. It is easier than ever before for an individual to make, create and contribute. Many people find that they cannot express their creativity at work, but the social realm provides a place where their ideas can make a real difference.

Polling data shows that each new generation feels less and less attached to the post-war welfare settlement. For the prewar generation, the very existence of the NHS remains a life-enhancing miracle. For many baby boomers, the welfare state was a starting point that should be expanded into a more comprehensive and responsive system. But for generations X and Y, brought up in a wealthier society with a less generous welfare state, and paying tuition fees that ensure they owe the state money for much of their adult lives, the welfare system does not look as compelling. More than two-thirds of those born before the Second World War believe that the creation of the welfare state was one of the country's proudest achievements, as compared to fewer than a third of those born between 1980 and 2000.[8] This is not a sign of selfishness or even of active rejection of the 1945 settlement. It is simply a lack of connection to big institutions of any kind and a spirit of self-reliance. Brigitte Kratzwald, an Austrian commons activist, sums up the ethos that runs through much of the commons movement:

> In many cases, governments have proven to be poor trustees of the things entrusted to them. Discontent about how they are doing their job is on the rise. People are standing up and taking responsibility with the words 'this is ours and we want to make the decisions about it'. Only through this process are these things becoming truly public goods and services.[9]

The idea of the commons as a form of self-governing mutual aid is already becoming a reality in some parts of Britain. It is visible in the huge number of new cooperatives that have been founded since 2010. The sector has grown by 26%, driven in part by a supportive policy environment that has helped communities to bid to run local assets such as pubs and post offices, and also by a growing enthusiasm for community cooperatives and the accumulation of greater experience in how to make them work.[10]

Energy Brixton, a company funded by investment from local people and governed by shareholders, is currently putting solar panels on local roofs and using its profits to educate local people about energy efficiency. The Scottish village of Fintry did a deal with a wind farm developer to build an extra turbine and give it to the locals, with the money earned from the power generated being used to fund community development projects. In North Yorkshire, the people of Hudswell formed their own cooperative to buy and refurbish the closed pub that had been the heart of their community.[11] For examples that are closer to the original definition of a common, look to Britain's woodlands, where the number of social enterprises taking on and caring for land has more than doubled since 2010, or the transformation of British Waterways into the charitable Canals and Rivers Trust.[12] Some 64% of British adults believe that the British state has tried to do too much in recent years.[13] Now they are showing that there is an alternative.

This may all sound a bit like David Cameron's idea of the Big Society; indeed, a few of the examples cited above were made possible by Coalition government policy, but the similarities are superficial. The Conservative offer to voters amounted to 'we're going to cut your services, could you please volunteer to keep them open?' This uninspiring proposition came in 2010 and 2011, at a point when few members of the public had even noticed the cuts. There was very little money for the Big Society, and not a great deal of policy. The whole thing was supposed to be led by an unpaid adviser to the Prime Minister, with very limited support from the Cabinet Office. The policy was an eye-catching orphan. Unsurprisingly, it did not work. Over recent years volunteering has remained static and the proportion of people who feel they can influence decisions about their local area has fallen slightly, as has participation in civic life.[14] The reality of deep local budget cuts has overwhelmed policies aimed at giving people more control over the places where they live.

The idea of the commons is far more ambitious than Cameron's Big Society. It requires us to change the way we see the places where we live. Too many of us think that our duty to the public realm begins and ends when we write a cheque for our council tax. If we continue to feel that way, then Garrett Hardin wins and our places become overused, under-governed, tatty and unloved. Instead, we need to recognise that localities are the engine rooms of prosperity and well-being, something that we all have a stake in but that none of us owns. That means that we all, as citizens and as businesses, have to play a role in looking after them. That might mean volunteering, but the exciting thing about the idea of the commons is that it goes well beyond litter picking or showing people around a stately home. It requires a philosophical reframing of the way in which we see ourselves in society. Our conception of citizenship has been dominated by the idea of a contract of rights and responsibilities that we implicitly sign at birth. To be a citizen is to be legally situated within society. Commoners are not legally recognised, but defined by their relationships with others. They have rights because they contribute to the maintenance of an asset – social, intellectual or physical – along with their peers. In essence, a commons is the combination of a resource, the social community that manages that resource and the rules and practices they use to do so.

Where the Big Society asked people to step in and fix the problems of a declining public sector, the commons simply asks people to do more of the things they care about, recognising that more social and civic action generally has a knock-on benefit for government in the form of enhanced social capital, reduced isolation and the unexpected benefits that flow from enabling social innovation. The best examples are the ones like the Waiting Room, where people collaborate to unlock their own creativity and tap into underused social resources. The emerging sharing economy also offers huge opportunities for building commons by encouraging people to share everything, from each other's cars to their lawnmowers and tools. Crystal-ball gazers increasingly suggest that city governments will soon start to use business models borrowed from Zipcar to improve the quality of life for people in poorer areas, for instance by turning expensive assets like cars or tools into cheaper or even free subscription services.[15] The commons suggests that we give in order to get; by helping to create shared resources, we can directly benefit from the existence of those resources.

One of the best examples of this approach is the time-banking movement, which allows people to exchange an hour of their work for an hour of someone else's without money changing hands. This is not only a great financial leveller – a lawyer's hour is worth as much as a painter's – but also a way to create social capital by linking people together. The Rushey Green time bank in South-East London is connected to a GP surgery that refers

patients who need help or involvement in group activities. The Fair
Shares community time bank in Gloucestershire offers a form of
health insurance that means that any member who has an accident
will be visited by other participants and offered help with errands
and chores for two weeks after they return home from hospital.
Evaluations of time banks suggest time and again that they are
effective in reducing isolation and making people feel better.[16]

A few areas have taken a step further and directly linked the idea
of the commons to building a local social economy. The decade
since 2005 has seen a flourishing of alternative currencies like the
Brixton pound (B£), a set of brightly coloured notes emblazoned
with pictures of David Bowie in his Aladdin Sane phase. Where
crypto-currencies like Bitcoin are often seen as a way to avoid tax
and undermine governments, the B£ is a way to keep more of
the wealth created in Brixton circulating among local businesses.
It can be spent only at local businesses that accept the currency,
and many offer a discount in return. Council staff can choose to
have part of their salary paid in the currency. A similar project
in Nantes, in France, is creating a new currency that amounts
to a barter system, allowing local businesses to offer one another
credit within pre-set limits, paid electronically in a unit called
SoNantes. A number of countries have launched similar initiatives
aimed at stimulating their local social economies. Brazil's Banco
Palmas offers emergency loans in a complementary currency and
Cleveland's major public sector institutions use their buying power
to support a network of cooperatives based in deprived areas,
providing laundry services and locally grown food.

Many of these ideas have their roots in a small Austrian village. In
the 1930s the mayor of Worgl, Michael Unterguggenberger, faced
high levels of unemployment and a pressing need for municipal
infrastructure but had only 40,000 schillings in the bank. He was
familiar with the work of the economist Silvio Gesell on alternative
currencies and decided to put it to the test. The schillings were
deposited in a local bank and used to back a system of stamp
payments. The stamps worked on a use-them-or-lose-them basis.
If they were not spent quickly, their value dropped precipitously.
Unterguggenberger used the stamps to pay for his project, but the

real magic lay in the rate at which the money circulated among local people. By keeping value circulating in the local economy, Worgl was able to start tackling unemployment far more quickly than many other Austrian towns. People paid their debts and taxes on time and the idea was picked up by neighbouring towns and villages. Some 200 other communities were ready to copy Worgl before the Austrian central bank stepped in to assert its monopoly on printing money.

Business should also be a critical player in growing the commons – after all, companies benefit from them too. With many large companies trying to demonstrate their social value, the strict lines that once divided public, private and voluntary are becoming blurred. A commons-based approach suggests that companies should be encouraged to put their money and expertise into the commons, and perhaps even have a role in governing those commons, so long as they do not try to enclose resources that should be freely available. The Benefit Corporation movement may provide the basis for a new level of private commitment to the commons. It brings together companies like Ben & Jerry's, Etsy and Patagonia, which are required to meet high standards of openness and transparency. Imagine a Commons Corporation equivalent that set out how businesses would support the growth of shared resources in the places where those companies operated.

As all of this suggests, one of the critical questions for the commons is about its relationship with government and business. Is this sort of social action a spanner that we can use to fix broken public service systems, a hammer to break apart the welfare state or a wooden spoon, a consolation prize for people who have lost formerly state-funded services? To answer that question, we need to visit a hurricane-lashed New York in 2012.

2 How the anarchists saved New York

The Occupy movement is famous for a brief flourishing of activity in 2011, when a group of angry students and radicals took over New York's Zucotti Park and sparked a global movement that eventually saw camps springing up across the world. The whole thing ended in evictions and, often, in profound disillusion. But what is less well known is that many of the Occupy movements carried on in some form. In New York, for instance, they formed groups to defend people threatened with eviction. But the most remarkable offshoot from the movement is surely Occupy Sandy, the moment when a group of anarchists and radicals became a fully fledged disaster-relief organisation.[17]

Superstorm Sandy was the second-costliest storm in American history, causing an estimated $65bn of damage and claiming 159 lives across 24 states. New York and New Jersey were hit particularly hard. Disasters are special moments. For those directly affected, they are often catastrophes, destroying cherished homes, causing displacement and misery that can change and disrupt people's lives for years to come. But what happens after a disaster can be extraordinary; survivors sometimes find that old social distinctions collapse, property and hierarchy become less important and, for a brief period at least, there can be joy and solidarity amid the destruction. The writer Rebecca Solnit has written movingly of how disasters like the 1906 San Francisco earthquake led to the creation of street kitchens where food was shared freely among the city's people. The radical social activist Dorothy Day was among those living in the city when the quake hit, and the experience inspired her to a life of passionate activism among the poor that would lead, years later, to her being considered for canonisation. 'While the crisis lasted, people loved each other,' said Day.[18]

Something extraordinary happened in New York too. After the storm hit, a group of Occupy activists drove out to the damaged neighbourhoods of Red Hook in Brooklyn and Rockaway in Queens to assess the damage and see what help people needed. They started posting online requests for space to cook food and for help with building a website, and set up a WePay account for donations. At this point, they were aiming to mobilise about 40 volunteers and perhaps a few hundred dollars' worth of donations, but things were going to get very much bigger. The Occupy group rapidly discovered that it needed more space, and started working with local activists to open a larger centre in Red Hook. A day later, Red Hook was overwhelmed with donations and volunteers and the Occupiers had to find yet more space at a church in the Sunset Park neighbourhood, which became their main distribution centre. A week after the storm, Occupy Sandy had gathered together around 700 volunteers and was serving about 20,000 meals a day. The number of volunteers eventually peaked at 60,000. All this from a network of people with no disaster-relief experience, who organised themselves through Facebook and Twitter at a time when some local offices of the Federal Emergency Management Administration (FEMA) were closing their doors in the face of continuing bad weather.

Occupy Sandy was, inevitably, a rough-and-ready sort of organisation. Volunteers would turn up at a church, write their name on a piece of tape and stick it to their clothing, then undergo a brief induction process, including sensitivity training and coaching for going door-to-door in disaster-stricken areas. The notes on the Facebook page ranged from an urgent request for generators to offers of free ear acupuncture for disaster victims. A typical instruction for a new volunteer would be a shouted: "If you have a car, you should cluster up and go see Alexis in the shearling hat."[19] The sheer pace of Occupy Sandy, combined with the need to organise such a wide range of different people and resources, was exhausting but effective. When one member realised that too many items were being donated that were not needed, he spontaneously set up an Amazon gift registry to help donors buy the most useful items and allow the distribution hubs to request surplus supplies from each other.

The whole initiative was grounded in the horizontal networking approach that had sparked the Zucotti Park sit-in in the first place. Traditionally, anyone who wants to help after a disaster has either to just offer money or to wait a few days until they can plug in to traditional state-run operations. Occupy offered something completely different: an attractively presented, easy-to-access approach to helping your neighbours by just turning up, undergoing rapid training and then contributing whatever skills you had, whether cooking or legal support. A large number of young, tech-savvy people in New York had nothing else to do after the storm hit. Occupy gave them a purpose. It also filled gaps in the traditional approach to disaster relief in the US. FEMA offered people loans to rebuild; the Red Cross offered medical help but could not reach everyone who needed it. Free from the constraints of regulation, Occupy volunteers would go into apartment blocks that others would not visit, and volunteer doctors would write prescriptions for people who needed critical drugs, in full knowledge of the fact that they could be personally liable if something went wrong. Among the key principles that underpinned all of this was the same one that informs Annemarie Naylor's Waiting Room: Occupy Sandy was not about charity but about mutual aid. It was about people helping one another as equals.

Of course, not everything was perfect. As with the original Occupy Wall Street, the governance of the money raised to support the relief effort became controversial. Nearly eight months after the hurricane struck, relationships with survivors in the Rockaway neighbourhood were getting testy as it turned out that about 20% of the funds raised by Occupy Sandy had not yet been spent. Agile, horizontal organisations do not always have the best book keeping, especially when they are trying to help in a hurry. The initiative was nonetheless taken seriously enough by the Department of Homeland Security that it commissioned a lengthy study of Occupy, concluding that it had highlighted important gaps in the federal plans for disaster relief and that FEMA needed to think more about how to incorporate horizontal local efforts into its strategies.

This may point the way towards the most fruitful kind of relationship between the state and the commons. Occupy Sandy was hardly a wooden spoon or a hammer. Rather, it acted like a spanner, working independently of formal state structures but drawing on support from them, including hot food from the Red Cross and advice from FEMA, and highlighting problems in traditional disaster response. The challenge for the future is not for the federal or city government to find a way to replicate Occupy Sandy – civil servants and self-organised, anarchist communities seldom mix well. Instead, it is to find a way to create a new kind of partnership between the state and society.

3 How Bologna gave the city back to the people

Bologna too has had more than a little experience of anarchists. The Italian city is sometimes known as the home of the fat, the learned and the red, and it has elected communist mayors for much of the post-war period. In the late 1970s one of those communists lost control of the city for three days as autonomist students took over the streets. The city's politics are much calmer today than they were during the so-called 'years of lead', but even if it's a lot more pragmatic these days, Bologna remains a city wedded to radical thinking and today it is becoming the first community in the world to embrace the idea that a city can be a commons.

It began at a seminar in December 2011. Christian Iaione is an Italian public contracts and procurement lawyer who encountered the idea of the commons while conducting research in the US. His work at New York University had applied the 'tragedy of the commons' to the problem of urban traffic congestion, calling for a more bottom-up approach to regulating traffic flows.[20] 'What I realised was how poorly we were working on exploiting the full potential of citizen innovation. The capacity of individuals, groups and neighbourhoods to innovative public policies,' says Iaione. 'I thought this was the way in Italy, the door I could open.' On his return home, he set out to turn the theory into practice.

Iaione had been asked to prepare a presentation about commons for a local foundation, and the director general of the Bologna city government was in the room. The meeting led to a two-year project in which the city's staff were trained to spot and engage with potential commons-based projects. Three labs were selected in different parts of the city and projects were trialled with abandoned buildings, green spaces and public squares. The approach has since expanded to the point where 35 projects have been delivered involving around 600 volunteers and engaging as many as 21,000 citizens. Being a lawyer, Iaione became increasingly convinced that he had spotted a problem in the legal framework that governed the municipality. A new regulation was needed to provide a firm grounding for the new experiments and to remove a number of administrative bottlenecks that were slowing progress.

Bologna could not initiate new legislation, but it could adopt local regulations based on the Italian constitution, and section 118 said that the public sector should favour citizens willing to take the initiative to carry out activities of general interest.

On this basis, Iaione helped to draft a new regulation to govern the city's interaction with the commons.[21] A law is an odd way to think about commons, and Iaione himself is a little ambivalent about the way that the regulation is being enthusiastically taken up by other cities. The point is the process of collaboration, not the legal format. But in practice the 26-page regulation covers a whole range of issues that vex attempts in Britain to work with communities, from questions about how the municipality should communicate with citizens (openly and using open source licences) to how risk should be handled (citizens have a duty to use suitable protective equipment). Whether underpinned by a law or not, the idea of the city as a commons continues to inform Bologna's attempts to reform itself in an era of austerity.

While citizens may not trust the government, they are starting to trust each other. In 2013 a Bologna resident called Federico Bastiani founded a phenomenon that came to be known as Social Street. Bastiani came from a small town in Tuscany where everyone knew each other and helped each other out. He wanted to create the same atmosphere around his home on the Via Fondazza and founded a Facebook page for his neighbours that rapidly grew until it had 500 subscriptions. Social Street has helped local people to share piano lessons and washing machines, and to organise street parties. There are 50 similar initiatives across Italy, with 20 in Bologna alone.[22] The idea has been acclaimed as the start of a new mutual aid economy, in which sharing and offering free support help people to save money. It builds on a strong tradition of mutualism in the private sector and in the way that the city delivers public services: 87% of social services are delivered by co-ops.

At the municipality, Michele D'Alena is one of those charged with spearheading the city's engagement with the commons. He envisages a future where a dedicated team at arm's length from the city helps to broker municipal support for commons-based projects, where government is "not playing the music, where we're more like a DJ, deciding what kind of music gets played". The city's first big project is to support a citizen-led initiative to save the San Luca porticos, a 3,796m long walkway running through the city, with frescos that are in danger of falling from the walls without sponsorship for much-needed conservation work. Says D'Alena:

> "There are not many examples for us to go on. We're trying to design something that does not exist yet. This is difficult to communicate because usually we start from our perfect project from the public administration but now we are releasing projects in beta version asking citizens to help improve it. If we empower the citizen, if we empower horizontal collaboration between citizen associations and enterprises, this project will become stronger than everything. It's not a project from a political party, it's a project that spreads in the city."

Bologna is beginning a project that could see the city become much less like the well-meaning but stuffy bureaucracy of municipal stereotype and more like a platform that supports people to do things for themselves. It is trying to become the sort of place where projects like the Waiting Room and Occupy Sandy can thrive, building on existing social capital and finding a way to work alongside the existing structures of government.

4 Leading the commons

In the UK we are surrounded by reminders of our declining democracy, from low turnout at elections to the precipitous decline in political party membership; from the nasty, boring and long 2015 general election campaign to the rise of populist parties on the Left and Right. Politics has become a game that is played out in the media a long way from the lived experience of most people's everyday lives. Indeed, some people claim that we no longer live in a mass democracy at all, but in a form of 'post-democracy'[23] that more closely resembles the royal courts of the 18th century, with politicians taking on the roles of the monarchy and aristocracy, and lobbyists playing the courtiers. At best, this is a world in which ordinary people are happy to have their voice represented by charities and pressure groups. We contribute to the political process by signing up to Greenpeace, going on a protest march or supporting the TaxPayers' Alliance. At worst, it is a world where the business of power is a distant soap opera, a world in which the alleged use of the word 'pleb' or a throwaway comment about nuns can dominate political debate for days.

The solution on offer from most democracy activists is some form of participatory democracy: we must re-engage the public by letting them into the process of local government, or by working with them to redesign the way public services work. But how many of us really want to sit in a draughty hall, helping the council to set its budget or finding new ways to co-produce social care? This stuff is important: the public should be far more engaged in local decision making. But rather than asking people to come into a council and help the politicians make it work more effectively, shouldn't we be asking them what they want to achieve in their lives and putting the resources of the state behind that? The commons offers a compelling alternative: not a democracy of participation or consultation, but a democracy of the deed, an idea of citizenship that emphasises the creative contribution we can each make directly, as citizens, to the commons around us. Best of all, this is a conception of democracy that has a direct benefit for each and every one of us in the form of greater personal well-being: volunteering has clearly been shown to significantly raise people's subjective well-being.

A democracy of doing that places local social action at the heart of its idea of citizenship will be profoundly challenging for political and managerial leaders. It cannot be led in the same way as a council or a government. It is very hard to take political credit for social action. The commons is not about spotting, developing and scaling a few good ideas at the national level. We do not need an Occupy Sandy in every city. Instead, we need lots of initiatives like the Waiting Room, and to allow them to transform the way that government works. If we develop lots of small things, they will eventually add up to a big thing. But this is quite a hard idea for governments to work with: ministers and councillors inevitably prefer to support programmes that they can commission, manage and control, so as to ensure that they meet their own political goals. I was recently asked by one senior local government official how he could 'bend' local social action to fit his council's priorities. Do not expect the commons to flourish in his part of London any time soon. The whole point is to create a realm where the politicians' goals are not always paramount.

This does not mean that politics has no role to play in a democracy of doing. Government can and should create the conditions that allow for human flourishing: the commons cannot grow if the commoners cannot find a decent job, afford a house or have access to skills and training. Ministers also have a role to play in championing the values of the commons; for instance, by emphasising the importance of civic participation in the education system. This is the kind of strategic context setting where local and central government should take on a far more active role. Even if Chancellor of the Exchequer George Osborne can deliver on his plans for huge spending cuts the state will still deliver the vast bulk of public services and retain control of huge sums of money. The key role for politics over the coming years will be to encourage, fund and support the emergence of this new realm of non-state, non-market action. Politicians have a critical role in putting resources into the commons and monitoring what emerges so as to ensure that public services are capitalising on social action and ensuring that local people have fair access to services and social support. Just as importantly, politicians can help to persuade the private sector to play its own vital part, contributing its expertise and money to the commons. This is about a three-way partnership of equals to grow the social realm.

The problem is that the 30 years since 1985 have not equipped our politicians for this job. While Britain has some extraordinary local leaders, the bulk of our politics has become mired in managerialism and complexity. Our leaders no longer tell us grand stories about the kind of society we might become and our role in helping to make that society come about. Instead, they offer dribbles of new money for the health service, or endless restructurings of hospitals and schools. Most councillors see their job as being focused on taking decisions in the town hall, managing services and allocating budgets. Professor Colin Copus of De Montfort University offers an unkind but instantly recognisable sketch of the 'party person' in local politics as someone whose life is tied up in keeping the machinery of their chosen group going, offering total loyalty to their tribe.[24] For Copus, this creates the unhealthy situation where dissent and debate must always be kept within the party, ensuring that real political discussion is internal and what must emerge are clean, clear decisions for public consumption; the public see only the hardened, outward monolith of Labour or the Conservatives. His survey work suggests that most councillors are what we might call 'soft Burkeans', believing strongly in the principle of representative democracy with some limited space for public engagement. It is hard to imagine a worse approach to leading a world of networks and commons.[25]

There is nothing wrong with representative democracy: we elect politicians to take the decisions we find it too difficult to manage as communities. It is a thankless job that most of them do fairly well, most of the time. In any case, no one has yet developed a convincing alternative that could completely replace the principle of representation. It is a reasonably good way to manage the formal business of running social care or planning transport routes, but a lousy way to lead the growth of the commons, a process that requires politicians to share their power and inspire others to take it. They need to be able to tell a story about how people coming together and collaborating can help to create a better society. They need to legitimately capture, frame and communicate a story about the common good of a city, and show each of us how we can contribute. Most importantly, politicians need to show us how the big challenges facing society play out in our everyday lives, and vice versa, and then give us the space to make change happen.

The futurist Vinay Gupta has devised a law of networked politics that states that in a networked environment the person who knows what to do next is in charge. That sums up both the power of a commons-based approach and the challenge. Political leaders are able to draw on a far wider range of ideas, skills and expertise than ever before, but in order to use those resources they must be prepared to openly share their power and to step back when someone else emerges who knows what to do next. If a councillor uses Twitter to get advice on taking a decision, then she needs to be prepared to debate the issue and explain how she subsequently voted. Politicians need to get used to sharing their evidence base, reasoning in public and trading political autonomy for a deeper sense of public engagement and democratic legitimacy. The hallmarks of the new leadership are promiscuous relationship building, open discussion and improvisation. This is why some of the most effective leaders of the post-financial crash period have been comedians. Men like Italy's Beppe Grillo and Iceland's Jon Gnarr have grasped that irreverence can be both populist and inspirational. Many of today's British politicians are inspired by figures like Churchill and Kennedy. In a democracy of doing, they have just as much to learn from stand-ups and artists.

One example of this sort of leadership is the tenure of Edi Rama as mayor of Tirana, in Albania. A shaven-headed former artist with a bohemian air gained in the galleries of New York and Berlin, Rama inherited a bankrupt municipality with almost nothing left in the coffers. His response: buy a load of brightly coloured paint and use it to revive the city. Many of Tirana's buildings still had a distinctly Soviet air about them, grey, tattered and lifeless. Rama chose one of them and painted it bright orange. The effect on the city was electrifying. Traffic jams formed around the building as people slowed down to take a look. EU officials threatened to deny Rama regeneration funding because the orange colour did not meet European standards. 'The surroundings do not meet European standards,' replied Rama.

Painting a building may not sound like a big deal, but in post-communist Tirana the vivid splashes of pink, yellow, green and violet combined with tree planting, new parks and road widening to help create a wave of pride and engagement with the fabric of a city that was previously decaying and full of poorly constructed illegal buildings. As Rama said: 'We noticed change. People started to drop less litter in the streets, for example, started to pay taxes, started to feel something they had forgotten, and beauty was acting as a guardsman where municipal police, or the state itself, were missing.'[26] The fabric of a city is a commons. Edi Rama created the conditions in which people could understand that for themselves, and take action about it, and he did it with cans of paint.

A declining state does not have to mean an impoverished society. It just means that we need to focus less on government and more on a whole range of socially useful activity that takes place across the whole economy. The best possible outcome from austerity is a world in which both the public and private sectors shrink a little, making more room for a whole constellation of social enterprises, community activism, more-than-profit business and cooperatives. This is a sector that is entirely capable of making money and producing economic growth, but does it with one eye firmly on building and maintaining the civic commons. It may also be a world where politics has to loosen up. Many of the challenges of the 20th century could be solved by policy, but those of the 21st are just as likely to be solved by performance, story-telling and inspiration.

FIVE

The colonisation of Britain: how the empire came home

Bermondsey in the early 20th century was squalid. Overcrowded, riddled with disease and reliant on the insecure work that could be got at the Surrey Docks. It was, in other words, the sort of place that attracted socialists. When Dr Alfred Salter and his wife, Ada, settled there in the 1910s and determined to make things better, the best tool available to them was the tiny Bermondsey council. When Labour took control of the council in 1922 it marked the beginning of a remarkable period of municipal experimentation that would see this impoverished 1,500-acre pocket of South London pioneer the basics of a free health service.[1] Dr Salter's Labour Party turned a country house into a convalescent home for new mothers, sent tuberculosis sufferers to Switzerland for solar treatment and eventually built a solarium in Bermondsey itself. The council gave lectures in schools on hygiene and diet. Three 'cinemotor' vans were constructed to show public health films in open spaces, taking their power from modified street-lamps. The facilities were funded almost entirely by local people, who paid rates that were twice as high as those in neighbouring boroughs. Their investment bought facilities so good that by the late 1940s they proved too expensive for the new NHS, which was forced to shut them down.

Alfred and Ada almost certainly did not know it, but they were taking power in Bermondsey at the beginning of a sort of localist golden age. In the opening decades of the last century councils created most of the components of a functioning welfare state, coming to manage everything from poverty relief to power generation, from adult education to the emergency services. At its height, local government in London accounted for 80% of the water supply, 70% of hospital beds, two-thirds of electricity generation and 40% of gas manufacture. The London County Council (LCC) ran 40,000 of the 55,000 general hospital beds in the capital and raised three-quarters of its own funding locally.[2] It was a time of vast energy and experimentation in the provision of a still-evolving set of public services.

Before its theft in 2011, Dr Salter's statue sat on a bench by the Thames, watching the brass figure of his daughter at play.[3] Her death from scarlet fever was the great price that he paid for his work in Bermondsey. The borough spread out behind him is now unrecognisable. Parts of the working-class community that the Salters served are still there, but they share their borough with artists, creative industries, migrants of every kind and a Surrey Docks that has become an unattractive out-of-town shopping centre. The old, Victorian town hall has become an imposing development of luxury flats, long replaced by the London Borough of Southwark's modern Tooley Street offices. Set among the gleaming headquarters of the Greater London Authority and PricewaterhouseCoopers, the offices are modern, light and airy. They are also part of a cost-cutting exercise that has allowed the council to close down and sell off older buildings as the council faces the rigours of austerity.

Southwark does not provide power to its residents. Neither does it run their schools, hospitals or colleges. It does not even raise very much of its own money. Where the pre-war LCC collected 77% of its budget from local people, Southwark raises less than 25%. The borough's leader, Peter John, is determined that the present decade of austerity will not just mean the orderly management of decline. His council is doing its level best to find innovative ways to handle the cuts that it faces. But seen from the historical perspective, it is hard to avoid the conclusion that a good deal of the decline has already happened.

This chapter tells the story of how the devolved world of the Salters became the centralised world of Peter John. It is a tale that spans little more than single generation, and that is dominated by two events: the creation of the welfare state and the battles between Margaret Thatcher and the new urban Left in the 1980s. There was nothing inevitable about the process. The British are no more centralist by temperament than anyone else, their geography no more unique than that of other countries. There is no special reason why Britain's welfare state has to be more centralised than those of practically any other comparable country. The story is one of accidental centralism: of two generations of radical politicians trying to reshape the world and removing the obstacles that they found in their way with remarkable ease. Central dominance emerged from the ways in which politicians chose to resolve the challenges they faced, not from the challenges themselves. At every juncture, localised solutions were possible. We drifted to the centre through choice, not destiny.

1 From municipal socialism to welfare state

Britain's devolved approach to public services grew out of a deep historical attachment to the local. A certain strand of Victorian British public opinion harkened back to the supposed liberties of the Anglo-Saxon age, when governance was managed by gatherings of the local great and good in the ancient woods of England. The roots of the country's decentralised culture were probably much more recent, lying in the Glorious Revolution of 1688, which replaced government by absolute monarchy with the governance of a cohesive aristocracy and gentry that met regularly in London before returning home to run the shires and boroughs. The 19th century saw the rise of the great municipal corporations, and the latter half of the century saw them flourish. The British have always had an ambivalent relationship with the urban, hymning the dynamism of city economies while worrying about the way they concentrate poverty and social pathologies. It was not surprising that urban governments tried to harness the former as a means to address the latter.

In Birmingham, the nonconformist preacher George Dawson would create a theology that became known as 'the civic gospel', a strand of thought that argued that the city was a more authentic

community than a nation, and that it should therefore be the place
where health, progress and fairness were achieved. His ideas would
come to fruition when Joseph Chamberlain took power in the city,
buying the gas-works and using the income to reshape the fabric
of the city. It would lay the foundations for municipal socialism.[4]
Parliament wanted to avoid taking a direct stake in local services,
so when central grants began to grow out of control they were
replaced by allocating several national taxes to the local level,
including alcohol excise duty.[5] The aim was explicitly to avoid
the encroachment of the centre into local affairs.

At this point in British history there existed what has been called
a 'dual polity'.[6] The primary concerns of Parliament were matters
of empire and war. The minutiae of domestic policy were left to
the great and good of the shires and, from 1835, to the emerging
local authorities. Of course, things were not quite that simple.
The Victorian city thronged with centrally mandated panels and
boards running poor relief and education independently of the
corporations. The early 20th century was a moment when the
need for a welfare system had become abundantly clear, but the
central state had yet to respond. In Bermondsey, Alfred and Ada
Salter filled the gap, but their Fabian socialist tradition could not
ultimately tolerate the mess and inconsistency of pre-war public
services. The Great Depression convinced the Labour movement
and many others that the dual polity could no longer stand.

Even so, it was far from obvious that the welfare state had to be
devised and run by the departments of state in London. Sidney
and Beatrice Webb had declared in 1921 that there were 'obvious
reasons why many industries and services have to be municipalized
rather than nationalized'.[7] The Beveridge Report, which became
the founding document of the 1945 settlement, suggested a big role
for friendly societies and trade unions – the working classes' own
self-help organisations – in managing sickness benefit. The People's
Will, as Beveridge became known, joined a broad consensus in
favour of a national health service to replace the jumble of council,
voluntary and private provision, but he was silent on exactly what
form it should take. As early as 1939, the officials of the Department
for Health were sending each other memoranda debating the

need for change after the war. The Permanent Secretary, Sir John Maude, tended towards expanding either national health insurance or municipal services, while Sir Arthur MacNalty, the Chief Medical Officer, tended towards nationalisation. A third view argued for groups of county councils to form joint boards to plan provision by the municipal and voluntary hospitals. In the final event, the Coalition government's 1944 White Paper put ministers in charge of planning the service but allowed councils to keep their executive function in running hospitals.[8] Indeed, Labour Party policy going into the 1945 general election was for the municipalisation of healthcare.[9]

By the time Aneurin Bevan came forward with his plans for the NHS in 1946, it was clear that Labour wanted to nationalise gas, electricity and perhaps also passenger transport and water. Bevan had concluded that the same must happen in healthcare. The voluntary hospitals – supported by donations – would have to receive the bulk of their income from the state in order to make the new national health service work. They would hardly be independent. The municipal hospitals were often too small to deliver high-quality care and could not be supported entirely through the rates. It was better to start with a clean slate and redesign the whole service with the help of medical professionals, Bevan argued. Besides, the doctors themselves were unlikely to consent to becoming local authority employees.

The debate about the creation of the NHS came to a head in cabinet when Bevan faced opposition from Herbert Morrison, the Labour Party's deputy leader who had made his name leading the LCC in the 1930s. Where Bevan saw a nationalised system that would bring order to the chaos of the pre-war health landscape, Morrison saw an assault on democracy. The Health Secretary's proposed regional management boards, staffed by Bevan's appointees, would inevitably become creatures of the centre. At the same time, they would fatally weaken the local authorities. This was more than just a question of Morrison protecting his former turf against encroachment. A point of principle was at stake:

> It is possible to argue that almost every local government
> function, taken by itself, could be administered more
> efficiently in the technical sense under a national system,
> but if we wish local government to thrive as a school of
> political and democratic education as well as a method
> of administration – we must consider the general effect
> on local government of each particular proposal. It would
> be disastrous if we allowed local government to languish
> by whittling away its most constructive and interesting
> functions.[10]

It is Bevan who is more often remembered as the romantic figure
of the Left, battling for socialist idealism against Hugh Gaitskell and
the later Attlee. But in the creation of the NHS his was the voice
of the men whom Rudolph Klein describes as the paternalistic
rationalists, the neat-minded medics and civil servants who wanted
order and tidiness. Some have gone as far as to argue that the
health service was a triumph both for socialists and for 'radical
managerialism'. From health to energy, the men who created
the post-war welfare state were the same men who governed an
empire. After the war, as their empire faded, they broke down the
barrier between the two polities, made common cause with the
Fabian socialists and colonised their own country.

Against this, Morrison offered a view of local government as
the foundation stone of democracy, a place where citizenship
was learned and the ability to take decisions together could be
fostered. It was a view that he would continue to fight for even
after 1946, encouraging the LCC to challenge Bevan in public
and in the courts. Needless to say, Morrison did not carry the day.
His arguments for democracy could not be forged into a strong
enough case to convince Attlee, who summed up the cabinet
meeting strongly in favour of Bevan's NHS. The impact on local
public services was profound.

Of course, the Conservatives objected. Geoffrey Hutchinson, a
Tory MP then between seats, wrote that 'everything which the
Labour government have done since they have been in power
indicates their preference for highly-centralised, non-democratic

methods of administration'.[11] Councils also found themselves despairing of their future. In 1946, Alderman J.W.F. Hill, the mayor of Lincoln, could point to 12 standing committees on his council, each taking decisions on different policy areas. Labour would abolish the transport, gas, electricity and public assistance committees, and perhaps also the water committee. The watch committee and the housing committee were, he felt, already agents of central government and the health committee had lost most of its functions. Alderman Hill was left with the works committee, the finance committee, parks, markets and cemeteries.[12]

If local government was a school of political education, then it was increasingly one with leaking roofs and mobile buildings for classrooms. It was not just councils that found themselves swept aside in the tide of centralism. While voluntary action burgeoned in the decades after the foundation of the welfare state, certain types of organisation struggled to find a new role. One example of what was lost could be found in the shape of the Pioneer Health Centre in Peckham, a remarkable experiment to which up to 950 working-class families subscribed, paying a small subscription for a mix of swimming, exercise, games and workshops. This was all observed by doctors who were keen to establish how social medicine could help to keep people well. The centre was once hailed as the greatest social experiment of its time, but its doctors felt that they were out of step with a health service focused on treating the sick. When the centre closed in 1950, due to lack of funds, its co-founder Dr Innes H. Pearse would say 'This is a true health centre, not an ill-health centre, and it is the only one in the world.'[13]

It is not quite true to say that the later 1940s and early 1950s saw a backlash against the welfare state, but they certainly saw some searching questioning as to what the Attlee governments had really achieved. Morrison's argument about schools of democracy had not gone away. Indeed, many within the party started to worry that they had defined their socialism too tightly in economic terms, focusing on making the working class better off but losing the moral idealism of the ethical socialist tradition.

One of the first to enter the lists was Michael Young, the head
of the Labour Research Department, who had penned the party's
1945 election manifesto. His heterodox education at the progressive
Dartington School, the only one in Britain to put fruit farming
on the curriculum, had developed a brilliant if wayward mind. He
wrote a memo in 1949 that argued that eliminating poverty was
not enough because 'the more you have [the] more you want'. He
wanted future Labour Party policy to focus on human relations,
arguing that child welfare centres should be concerned with
emotional as well as physical needs, that government should set
up marriage guidance centres to reduce divorce and that the party
should aim to improve the quality of life in its broadest sense. He
poured scorn on the idea that all that socialism needed in order to
flourish was 'total abstinence and a good filing system'.[14] Young
would eventually leave the Labour Party to become a sociologist
and social entrepreneur, founding endless organisations that would
make his vision of a bottom-up, decentralised socialism a little bit
more real.

His views were far from the fringes. As early as 1947, Labour's
National Executive Committee had commissioned Young to write
a discussion paper on how the benefits of large industrial and social
structures could be combined with the benefits of 'smallness'.
Tony Crosland had urged that Labour should return to the 'moral-
cultural-emotional appeal of the William Morris tradition'.[15] In
1955, Richard Crossman would criticise the nationalised industries
for not being properly accountable to Parliament and not giving
their workers a share of management. 'The growth of a vast,
centralised state bureaucracy constitutes a grave potential threat
to social democracy,' he claimed.[16] Much later, as shadow Health
Secretary, he would criticise his opposite number, Keith Joseph,
by declaring: 'I say to the secretary of state that his managerialism
is terrifying'.[17]

Even Bevan would recant. Writing in the *Municipal Journal* in
1954, he said that he now felt that the lack of an elected base for
the health service was a weakness in the system. His answer was a
reorganisation of local government to create large-enough councils
to manage the NHS. 'Machines are important, but democracy is

a way of life,' he declared. It was an idea that would resurface in
the late 1960s when local government and the health service were
both being reorganised. Both political parties agreed in principle
that returning the NHS to local government control would enable
far more effective integration of treatment, personal services and
prevention, even if they knew that in practice they could not
deliver such a major change to a cherished national institution.

  Yet it was not the end of local government. Councillors might
feel themselves diminished, but to a young Alan Bennett the great
and good of the post-war Leeds Corporation were still 'grand
and mysterious figures'.[18] Local government still raised around
two-thirds of its own money by 1950, and would continue to
raise a majority of its own income well into the 1970s.[19] When
Bevan spoke to audiences of aldermen and officers, he urged
them to be of good cheer. Had he not once been one of Britain's
youngest councillors? Had he not known all of the functions of
local government before the age of 25? In place of their previous
functions, there would be central grants, above all else for housing.
The country's housing stock had been decimated by the war and
Bevan wanted councils to build; a demand that would only intensify
during the 1950s.[20] The most visible role for local authorities over
the next 30 years would be the reshaping of towns and cities.

  The historian David Kynaston has provided a full survey of
all the rebuilding works carried out between 1960 and the
summer of 1962. They included a gigantic rehousing programme
in Birkenhead, the approval of plans for the redevelopment of
Blackburn's old market, a five-storey office block going up in front
of Bradford's railway station, a 'multi-storey crash drive' to develop
new housing in Brighton, the demise of the Empire Palace in Leeds
and many, many more. Some Tories worried about repeating some
of the same mistakes made during the rapid development of the
cities in the 19th century. Labour politicians were more gung-ho,
eager to replace slums that were taking far longer than expected
to clear. As Kynaston makes clear, it was local leaders who had
day-to-day control.[21]

  The Newcastle MP Edward Short opened a new block of
flats and declared: 'This surely is the dawn of a new epoch in the

forward march of mankind.' The council's leader, T. Dan Smith, was praised as 'one of the great builders of the city'. Just over a decade later Smith would be in prison, charged with accepting bribes from developers. Not everything went wrong – some of the municipal developments stood the test of time – and councils were not always responsible for the outrageous shortcuts taken by developers working in a hurry with tight budgets. But disasters like the Hulme Crescents had happened largely on the local authorities' watch, and, just as the public and politicians were starting to realise the full extent of the mistakes made in the 1960s, the party ended for the public sector.

Local government's fortunes had always been bound up with the state of Britain's cities. Britain's localised pre-war welfare state was a product of the success of the 19th-century municipal corporations in adapting what were often absurdly overgrown towns into the powerhouses of the late industrial era. In contrast to the grand monuments of Victorian municipalism, local government's role in post-war reconstruction had often resulted in cheap, leaky brutalism.

As the 1970s oil shocks rocked the British economy, deindustralisation continued to gather pace and jobs fled from the cities, leaving poorer residents and decaying industries behind them. Some of this was the logical consequence of national policy: governments had been trying to disperse people from London and the other cities since the war, using the green belts to constrain urban growth and drive people out to new towns like Milton Keynes and Thurrock. This was an era when left-wing squatters could take over whole streets of abandoned houses in areas like Lambeth.

The Keynesian welfare system had promised the full employment that had been such a vital component of Beveridge's plan, and its collapse had suddenly brought worklessness back onto the agenda. For the first time in a generation, the cities badly needed jobs. The sheer pace of economic change combined with the oil shocks of the 1970s to put huge pressure on urban councils' budgets, driving up their costs while creating a huge demand for investment in new jobs and industries. Relationships between councils and the business community fractured under the strain. Michael Heseltine, the former Environment Secretary, has one word to describe the state of the cities when he came to power in 1979: 'appalling'.

2 The rate-capping rebellion

New York's mayor, Fiorella la Guardia, once said that there was no Democratic or Republican way to fix a sewer. He was wrong. Within certain circles in 1980s Britain, there was a left- and a right-wing way to do everything, especially in local government. For Thatcher's children, her victory over the local Left seems inevitable. At the time, it seemed anything but. Tony Benn could write of a coming battle between neoliberalism, corporatism and democratic socialism and be taken entirely seriously.[22] By 1988, the graphic novelist Alan Moore would use the preface to his classic *V for Vendetta* to provide a powerful summary of the cultural polarisation felt by many on the Left when he said of Britain: 'It's cold and it's mean-spirited and I don't like it here anymore.'

As the new Conservative government began reining in public spending, it would encounter furious resistance from some of the cities. The facts of the matter are straightforward. In 1984, concerned about rising rates, the government was in the midst of introducing legislation allowing ministers to cap the total amount that councils could levy. The new Labour administration in Liverpool decided that the budget it had inherited was not enough and demanded more money from the centre. After much pushing and pulling as the council tried and failed to set a legal rate, the Environment Secretary, Patrick Jenkin, capitulated and released £20 million more for housing.

Emboldened, many of the Labour councils that faced rate capping in 1985 followed suit and refused to set a rate. Working alongside the striking miners, their aim was to force the government to back down, releasing more funding and removing the capping powers. The miners had helped to force Edward Heath from power in 1974 and faced Thatcher down over pit closures in 1981. The idea that councils and colliers working together could break Thatcher was not quite as fanciful as it now seems. It nonetheless amounted to a revolutionary strategy, designed to use extra-parliamentary activity to break the government's whole economic approach. What the rate-cap rebels were doing was also illegal and it put Labour councils in the bizarre position of defending the working class by raising loans from foreign banks and putting local services at risk. "People had mistaken a shield for a sword," says Barry Quirk, then chairman of the rebellious London Borough of Southwark's finance committee.

The rebels were a high-profile minority within the Labour Party, but by flying what amounted to a kamikaze mission against the Thatcher government they provided the Tories with the perfect cover for a new wave of centralism. Local government would lose much of its role in housing, become the subject of a huge experiment in local taxation that would eventually halve their locally raised revenues, witness the abolition of a whole tier of urban local government in the form of the Greater London Council and its equivalents in the other big cities and, finally, see its reputation dragged through the gutter. Whether any of this was sensible or fair barely matters: local government had misplayed its hand and it would take 30 years to recover.

The Labour Party leadership deplored the whole approach. Neil Kinnock argued that it was better for Labour councils to remain in power as a 'dented shield' than to risk having their budgets set for them by government commissioners. 'Conflict is easy,' he told the party's local government conference to cries of 'Rubbish!': 'bullying is easy, but partnership is the tough one'.[23] Nor was local unanimity easy to maintain. In Manchester, the council leadership's attempt to join the rebels was blocked by a coalition of moderate Labour backbenchers and the Tory opposition. Several councils that did join the rebellion subsequently backed down because of similar backbench revolt against the leadership.

The whole mess collapsed as, one by one, each council gave in and set a legal rate. Those councillors who held out longest faced personal consequences. A total of 81 councillors from Liverpool and Lambeth were surcharged for the interest their councils had forfeited and disqualified from office for five years. Some left-wing authorities would manage to use a raft of financial trickery and rate rises to avoid redundancies while waiting for a Labour victory in 1987 that would deliver new public investment. When it failed to materialise, the game was up.

The conflict was underpinned by two uncompromising ideas of the future of Britain. For the neoliberal Thatcherites, local government was an impediment to the creation of a country based on the free market. Like the miners and the professions, the councillors had to be faced down. The Thatcherites had a point. Local authorities were huge, controlling around 40% of all government spending, housing almost a third of the population, employing more than 10% of the workforce and funded partly by local taxes that they could and did raise to offset central cuts. It was not clear to the Thatcherites that local elections could ensure efficiency, especially when poorer voters who paid little or no tax could vote for more services with few personal consequences. If cities wanted to resist the policies of the centre – and in the early 1980s many of them did – there was not much the centre could do about it.

This had to change if Thatcherism was to succeed. In a first wave of reform, councils lost much of their role in housing as grants were slashed and the Right to Buy substantially reduced the number of council houses. Capping was introduced to stop big rate increases. Later, councils would lose their control over the money they collected in rents, effectively stopping them from borrowing against their rental income to build new homes. Competitive tendering forced councils to put an increasing range of their services out to competition with the private, with decidedly mixed results. Most radically, the Thatcher government developed the idea of the community charge, now better known as the 'poll tax'. This was supposed to increase accountability, but it was equally an attempt to weaken Labour's grip on the cities. If the poor had to pay the same tax as everyone else, they could no longer vote for socialist councillors to make free with wealthier people's money. It would prove to be perhaps the most spectacular policy blunder of the past 30 years, and the fact that it was tested first in Scotland would contribute powerfully to that country's sense of grievance against Westminster.

Although the poll tax itself was defeated, the accompanying proposal to nationalise business rates stood. Thus was created a strange tax that could never rise in real terms, that was legally a local levy but in practice was collected by councils and sent to the Treasury to be redistributed. The effect was that business paid an ever-smaller share of the cost of local services. It is a very good deal when inflation is low, but a very bad one in recessions, when it tends to rise, due to government stimulus spending. In other words, central control of the business rate keeps it low in the good times and raises it in the bad.

Perhaps just as importantly, the Tories believed that Britain's cities should be regenerated through private investment. If left-wing Labour councils refused to work with business, then Whitehall would do it for them. Huge urban development corporations were set up to redevelop first Merseyside and then Manchester, the London Docklands and many other parts of the country, led by men and women appointed from Whitehall with a remit to bring business to the table. Socialist councils waiting for the funds to support public regeneration risked ending up on the side lines as towns and cities began a long process of transformation.

The Right had its own tradition of defying the centre – witness Tory resistance to the abolition of the grammar schools in the 1960s. In Westminster, the council used its housing policy to illegally change the demographic make-up of key electoral wards to secure a Conservative majority. It was not just the Left that played fast and loose with the law in the 1980s. The Right too had its own municipal radicals, determined to reshape their councils along Thatcherite lines. From the late 1970s onwards Wandsworth, in South London, put its services out to competition, reduced its staffing by a third and cut its tax bills.

If the Right was determined to destroy local government's ability to set its own social policy, the Left wanted to use it as a battering ram to bring down the Thatcherites and launch a change of direction. Some of those who lived through the period argue that the Conservatives were already set on a course towards central control and that the fight against the new urban Left was a sideshow. Even if they are right, there can be no question that the

rate-capping debacle and the so-called 'loony-left' helped to justify
Thatcher's behaviour in the eyes of the public. Even the relatively
moderate David Blunkett, then leader of Sheffield City Council,
would declare that 'socialism will not come from parliamentary
action alone'.[24] As Ken Livingstone put it after taking control of
the Greater London Council (GLC):

> No one will be in any doubt that the GLC is now a
> campaigning organ and a bastion of power for the Labour
> movement. Part of our task is to sustain a holding operation
> until such time as the government can be brought down and
> replaced by a left-wing Labour government.[25]

A spirit of insurrection had been brewing throughout the 1970s.
Marxist academics had started to explore local government's role
in reproducing capitalist labour relations, a terrifying phrase that
really meant nothing more than that councils tried to produce
educated and skilled workers. The Home Office's Community
Development Programme (CDP) was totemic. A scheme designed
to put action and research teams into local authorities to improve
morale in deprived areas, it became mired in debates about its
role and scope that resulted in a certain radicalisation. Many team
members in the 12 participating councils came to believe that
the problems of poverty that they were addressing were structural
and therefore lay beyond the CDP's remit. The teams turned their
efforts to critiquing central government policy, creating a central
unit to share their findings and releasing a report called *Gilding
the Ghetto*, which critiqued the CDP itself and condemned the
government's motivations in setting it up.[26]

David Regan, a professor of local government at Nottingham
University, used an influential pamphlet to describe a local Labour
movement in the grip of an odd mix of devolutionary guild
socialism that demanded municipal independence and a neo-
Marxism that saw councils as a tool for transforming society as a
whole.[27] His case was wildly overstated. The radical Left controlled
only a handful of councils. Most Labour authorities and the two
capped Tory councils of Portsmouth and Brent protested loudly,

then went about business as usual. Even within the Left, there were
only a few who might qualify as anything approaching Marxist,
and they were concentrated among the Merseyside militants and
within Ted Knight's Lambeth. What was really happening was a
rejection of men like T. Dan Smith and Harold Wilson, whom a
new generation of university-educated leftists like Manchester's
Graham Stringer blamed for the disappointments of the 1970s.

The radical Left dragged local government into a national fight
for the future of the country. Neil Kinnock had told the rebels
that it was better to have a dented shield than no shield at all. In
the event, the shield was crushed. Victory helped only to justify
and sharpen Thatcher's centralising instincts. As the 1980s turned
into the 1990s, the Labour Left started to lose ground to a new
generation of managerialists, who focused on securing better
and more efficient services instead of confronting the by-now
triumphant Thatcherites. But the damage was done. The 1980s left
their mark not only on local government but also on a generation
of Labour politicians. David Blunkett had been in the thick of
it in Sheffield, Tony Blair had wanted to stand as a councillor in
Hackney in the early 1980s. Michael Barber, who would go on
to lead Blair's delivery unit, got as far as the council chamber. It
left an unfavourable impression:

> I watched the madness around me and tried to vote sensibly.
> In fact, there was a minority of us in the Labour group whom
> the others described disparagingly as 'the sensible caucus',
> which left me wondering about what they were.[28]

It was not just the Right that had lost faith in the potential of the
local: it was the emerging Blairite tendency too. And they were
heading for power.

3 High managerialism

The first draft of history has described the Blair governments as
being some of the most centralising of the post-war era. But things
are never quite so straightforward. All governments contain conflicts

and contradictions. Thatcher believed in economic freedom but was politically centralising. Blair was a communitarian who had no patience with communities. In fact, his first term included some remarkable decentralisations, including the creation of the devolved administrations and the elected mayor of London. The New Deal for Communities spent a substantial amount of government money on funding local service providers to support community-led projects in Britain's most deprived neighbourhoods. Norman Glass, one of the creators of the Sure Start children's centres, would describe Sure Start's parent-led approach as 'anarcho-syndicalist'.

The former local government minister Nick Raynsford argues that the Blair years were characterised by a tension between the desire to decentralise power and the drive to deliver rapid change fuelled by the more centralising aspects of the Fabian socialist tradition. For him, the turning point was 2003. Raynsford was about to end council tax capping for the best councils, but before he could do so his department was rocked by an average council tax rise of 12.9% across the country. There were many reasons for this, but Raynsford remembers the Prime Minister being 'apoplectic' about the development. Not for the first time, local government had shot itself in the foot. Labour soon developed the idea of 'double devolution', which was supposed to mean handing power to councils and, beyond them, to communities. In practice, says Raynsford, it was used to justify cutting councils out of the loop entirely.

A mix of what Professor Christopher Hood termed 'targets and terror' was to become the order of the day. It became too much for a few New Labourites. Geoff Mulgan, who headed Blair's strategy unit, would leave the government in 2004 to revitalise Michael Young's Institute for Community Studies. His reasons were simple: "I thought the view from the centre became distorted – hubristic about how much change could be centralised, dictated, specified."

The results were mixed, as we have already seen. The range and quality of health services were transformed by a huge financial injection, but the longer-term future of the NHS was not secured, because of the lack of priority placed on reducing the long-term costs of conditions like obesity. Child poverty was reduced significantly, but the dream of ending it remained elusive. Schemes were put in place to build new homes, but in practice not all of them were delivered. Local government was subjected to a hefty regime of inspections in which every aspect of its work was ranked into a single league table. Every local authority chief executive in the country dreamed of receiving a prized 'four stars and improving' rating from the Audit Commission.

Services got better, but it is not always clear that the public noticed. The focus on league tables certainly encouraged conformity above innovation, and the adoption of best practice that had secured a good ranking elsewhere, rather than the invention of radically different ways to deliver services. Academics such as Hood produced awkward evidence suggesting that at least some public services were 'adjusting' their data to meet targets and that in others the target produced perverse results.[29] Still, it was a better outcome than some New Labour thinkers had feared – in the mid-1990s they had assumed that Blair's Napoleonic tendencies would result in something like the abolition of independent local government altogether.

Labour took three ideas to their logical conclusion, exhausting their potential as levers of change. The first idea was centralisation, which is exhausted because there is simply no further to go. By the end of the Blair/Brown era, there was precious little left over which the centre could practically assume any further control. Seven pounds in every £10 of central government grants were ring-fenced for a specific purpose, and only a quarter of council revenue was raised locally. In a speech to the Institute for Government, Tony Blair made clear his belief that 'If you want to drive through systemic change, you've got to drive it through from the centre'.[30]

The second idea was managerialism: essentially, the philosophy of bringing private sector management disciplines into government. It is symbolised by the idea that there should be a 'line of sight' from the centre of government down to the front line, and by the McKinsey slogan that 'everything can be measured and what gets measured gets managed'. By 2010, there was simply no further to go with this idea – it is very hard to imagine a state more managerial than Britain at the height of Blairism. Managerialism created unintended consequences, encouraging public servants to manage the target rather than serve customers. As we have seen, simple top-down goals seldom offer a solution to complex social problems. One very senior servant described a 'cycle of despair' that faced the government in areas like teen pregnancy as more targets were set, more money was spent and yet the government still struggled to meets its goals.[31] The result was, too often, services that looked good on paper but that disappointed citizens. This might have been forgivable if managerial approaches had increased efficiency and productivity, but it is not always clear that they did.

The final, now exhausted, idea was Labour's particular tradition of bossy statism, which is deeply connected to the previous two strands of thinking. As Labour tried to find new ways to achieve outcomes, it increasingly started seeing the public themselves as an adjunct to the public sector. People's behaviour became another factor for government to manage through new criminal offences and regulations, while community and voluntary action was all too often instrumentalised as a mere tool for achieving government objectives. Between 1997 and 2007 the Blair governments dreamt up 303 initiatives designed to change public behaviour, with the Department of Health and the Home Office producing the most.[32] On some measures, Labour created a new criminal offence for every day it spent in office. The voluntary sector doubled in size on the back of state contracts that usually came with strings attached.

By 2010, centralism had run its course. Labour recognised this itself. The inspection superstructure was already being trimmed, its targets pruned and its costs reduced. The preceding 30 years had represented the apogee of the centralist experiment. It had run out of road.

4 Accidental centralists

The most popular explanation for British centralism has it that the development of a universal welfare state inevitably entangled local government in a web of national entitlements. On this reading, as councils moved away from providing public goods to the Victorian city and towards becoming a prototype welfare state, they were forced to accept more central government money that inevitably came with strings attached. Localism could not survive if it involved spending other people's money. Michael Heseltine has put this case succinctly:

> A long democratic process rightly tackled the consequences of urban squalor and often acute poverty. But in the process local initiative gradually moved from the enterprising industrialists to the councillors of today – much more preoccupied with a social agenda than earning the wealth to pay for it. And as the costs of such social provision relied increasingly on central government, so a range of circulars, ring-fenced grants, hypothecated funding and a new breed of quangos further eroded local discretion. Local government assumed the character of Whitehall's branch offices.[33]

Our brief survey of the history suggests that Heseltine is, at best, only partly right. Men like Joseph Chamberlain were undoubtedly more swashbuckling than many of their modern counterparts, but they did not inhabit a prelapsarian world of liberated local government and their limited powers made many of them bystanders in the face of extreme poverty and deprivation. While it is certainly true that the creation of some form of welfare state was inevitable and that this would necessarily involve a degree of standardisation of local services, the form of that welfare state was hotly contested until the very last moment. A social policy expert living in the 1930s would probably have predicted a substantial development of municipal services, with national taxes used to ensure equal access and a degree of standardisation. Many other countries would show that such an approach could be made to work exceptionally well by creating highly decentralised welfare states, with health and benefit systems run by municipalities.

The centralisations of the 1980s were fundamentally the result of local government being on the losing side of a battle for the future shape of the British economy. Even this was not straightforwardly a fight between agendas that favoured either growth or welfare, but a battle about different ways to return a sclerotic economy to prosperity. The mainstream town hall Leftists wanted to use public investment to forge a path towards a new economy of worker ownership and decentralised planning. As Manchester's Graham Stringer puts it: "Prior to 1987 we had had a what you might call a municipal view of the world – a left-of-centre, Keynesian view that the problems of unemployment, poverty and poor service could be solved by taxation and public expenditure." It may sound unlikely today, but in the 1980s it was simply an extension of what governments had traditionally done during the post-war consensus.

Other countries dealt with the challenges of recessions and financial crises very differently. At the same time as Margaret Thatcher felt compelled to clip the wings of British councils, François Mitterand was embarking upon a programme of decentralisation that he described as *la grand affaire du septennat*, or the chief task of his seven-year term. When Sweden faced a financial crisis in the early 1990s that required it to cut back public spending, it actively decentralised, giving up many central controls on local government grants. Denmark has adopted a decentralised model that pushed welfare down to the level of local authorities, in large part so as to drive efficiency by confronting local people with the trade-offs between different policy options. Councils are responsible for a very large proportion of GDP, but overall spending is controlled by agreements between the finance ministry and the Danish local government association, resulting in a system that has combined decentralisation with tight spending controls, if not perhaps the strongest system of political accountability.[34]

Britain's centralism is ultimately a result of political ideology and managerial convenience, not of grand historical forces. Labour and the doctors favoured nationalisation. Thatcher was looking for an opposition to crush, and local government stepped enthusiastically into her trap. In other countries, the constitution would have put a break on this. Federal states such as those found in Australia or Germany would have been able to dampen the force of Attlee or Thatcher's parliamentary majorities. A constitutional clause setting out the role of local government and its relations with the centre might have forced a wider debate about the consequences of change. But in Britain, sovereignty lies in Parliament, and

Parliament is dominated by an executive that wants to get its own way. In this context, questions about the local inevitably come back to efficiency and convenience, rather than democracy and collaboration. Today, it appears as if the grand, centralist experiment is coming to an end. This is partly because the Blairites tested it to destruction and left the opposition – and indeed a future Labour government – with nothing else to centralise. It is partly because the political class has come to realise that the future of Britain's economy is bound up with the success of its generally underperforming regional cities, which need more power and investment if they are to thrive. The demise of high centralism is also deeply related to wider social currents: a more assertive and capable population, disillusionment with Westminster politics, the constitutional crisis sparked by the Scottish referendum.

But it is also because local government appears to have learned the lessons of the past 30 years. Council services are arguably better managed than ever before. Faced with cuts even deeper than those of the 1980s, left-wing local authorities have wisely focused on innovative new approaches to getting things done, rather than campaigning against austerity. Today's city leaders are pragmatic social entrepreneurs: Southwark's Peter John rightly sees himself as following in the footsteps of Dr Salter, rather than of the radicals who led his council in the 1980s. And as we have seen, the local wins allies when it is seen as pragmatic and problem solving. The stage is set for a long process of change as we reshape British government for the 21st century. A revolution is coming. It will not be easily achieved – giving power away can be difficult even when you want to do it – but the one thing we do know is that it will not be centralised.

SIX

Giving up is hard to do: why politicians struggle to share power

In 2010, David Cameron issued an 'invitation to the people to join the government of Britain'. The words were embossed on a hardback election manifesto full of promises to reverse the centralism of the Blair years and usher in a wave of new powers to set up schools, take over public assets, tailor planning for neighbourhoods and bid to run council services. Downing Street staff claimed that their favourite book was Fritz Schumacher's *Small is Beautiful*, with its chapters on the Buddhist economics of happiness and its call for decentralised industries and public services. The Prime Minister's adviser, Steve Hilton, cycled into work wearing a T-shirt printed with the words 'big government' accompanied by a frowning red emoticon next to a glowing, smiley-faced 'big society' logo. And yet the public seemed curiously unwilling to reply to that beautifully presented invitation. The hardbacks were used as coasters and props for wobbly desk legs, an invitation awaiting an RSVP that never came.

The results of Cameron's first-term drive for decentralisation are a decidedly mixed bag. While Greater Manchester made big strides towards securing its freedom, it is an exception among the regional cities, most of which have seen only modest devolution of economic powers and very few new responsibilities for public services. Indeed, some areas of social policy became considerably more centralised under the Coalition government, particularly those concerned with welfare and worklessness. Councils were offered incentives to freeze their tax and forced to hold referendums if they wanted more than a token increase, eroding local financial control to a point from where it may be hard to return. Mutuals and cooperatives do seem to have flourished, but on most measures the Tory promise of a bigger society has not increased social action.[1] Michael Gove's free schools were designed to empower parents, but they have done just as much to empower the Department for Education. Cameron's Coalition government proved keen to devolve responsibility for cutting public services, but less so to share real power and responsibility with local people. England is probably a more decentralised place than it was in 2010, but only very slightly, and not in ways that many members of the public will have noticed.

This partly reflects a series of paradoxes at the heart of the way that the Conservatives were thinking about localism. On the one hand, they wanted to liberate local authorities and communities from bureaucracy; on the other, they wanted to restrain their freedom of action. Councils got fewer targets, but lost a substantial chunk of their budgets, their residual role in education and much of their ability to set local taxes. The government introduced a Localism Act that did not include any substantial new freedoms for local councils, but did grant the Secretary of State 145 new powers. Ministers wanted to decentralise more power over education and healthcare to the individual, giving them more choice about how they accessed their services, conveniently ignoring the fact that all the big decisions are democratic ones. Consumer choice can give me the ability to go to a different hospital, but it gives me no say in the larger question of the overall shape of the health system. Neighbourhood planning can give me the ability to make a new development look nicer, but it gives me no real say in the siting of an out-of-town shopping centre that could gut my local high street.

Politicians often say they want to give away power, particularly when they are in opposition. It is an inexpensive promise to make, and an attractive one too. No one wants to be seen as a power addict. Even politicians like Lord Heseltine, an arch-centraliser in his time, wince when the term 'centraliser' is applied to them. But in practice the promise to devolve is made more often than it is kept. This is not generally because national politicians are liars and frauds, but because giving power away is hard to do. Too often the risks seem to outweigh the benefits and ministers choose to invest their political capital elsewhere. Most governments default to calling for an incremental process of reform, claiming that a slow and careful process of devolution will eventually transform the country. In practice, the cracks in the current system are usually papered over and left to widen.

Perhaps the best example of this is the council tax. It was introduced in 1993 as a modern property charge to replace the disastrous poll tax. Estate agents across the country were paid to drive slowly down residential streets, sorting every home in the land into one of eight bands. The problems kicked in straight away. The Major government, which had introduced the new tax, used its capping powers aggressively to keep spending down. In 1997 Labour decided to use the powers more sparingly, but they remained in place and were used more and more often as the Blair years dragged on.

A big part of the problem is that the council tax was very poorly designed. It is palpably unfair: a millionaire living in a palace pays just three times as much as a young working family in a one-bedroom flat down the road. It is also a very bad way to fund public services. Many taxes rise with the economy. If you get a pay rise, then you automatically pay a little bit of it to the Treasury, but council tax is based on the value of your property in 1993, and that never changes. If inflation is at 2%, the local authority has to raise its tax by that amount just to stand still. The result is a very good deal indeed for the winners in the housing market, who have seen their wealth grow considerably while their tax bill remains static, but it is a bad deal for everyone else. David Cameron's Coalition government only complicated matters further. Councils were encouraged to freeze their bills and could raise them above 2% only by holding an expensive referendum. The council tax has become an annual bill that many of us assume never rises, controlled by a referendum that most local politicians assume they will never win. If this is still a local tax at all, then it has become a very peculiar one indeed.

The localist renaissance is fundamentally a process of bottom-up change: one that relies on local communities and institutions taking and exercising power for themselves. But local renewal will remain vulnerable as long as power is locked up in Westminster. We badly need the national elite to hand down serious new powers, and to convince them to do so we need strategies to counter the spiral of centralism and its associated culture of mend-and-make-do reform. If we really want a more decentralised country, we have to understand why giving up power is hard to do, but not impossibly so.

1 Breaking the grip of centralism

The British political system is not as democratic as we like to think. The historian W.G. Runciman has imagined a visit by the 18th-century author Daniel Defoe to modern Britain, and concluded that he would recognise the fundamental settlement: 'Neither the increase, however large, in the number of the state's employees, nor the extension, however intrusive, of the power attaching to their role, significantly altered the institutional distribution of political power.'[2]

Over several hundred years, we have replaced a monarch with a constitutional figurehead, but the power wielded by prime ministers is still that of the Queen in Parliament. Our political parties compete to form an executive that wields monarchical power and is held only partly in check by parliamentary sovereignty. The system is set up to be run from the centre, and the institutions that have evolved around it, from the media to the lobbying firms, are all set up on the same basis.

In this world, politicians take the blame for public service failure but generally do not receive any praise for success: for instance, 47% of us say that we would hold the government responsible if policing got worse, but if it gets better then 41% think it is the police that should take the credit.[3] This makes devolution very hard to achieve in practice. You cannot just pass power downwards without also creating new structures of governance and accountability to ensure that responsibility goes with it.

It requires a significant act of will for national politicians to break out of the spiral of centralism, and even then they cannot do it on their own: they need some measure of support from local political elites and from the public themselves.[4] This kind of alignment is often hard to manufacture. This is not to suggest that politicians are simply the helpless victims of broader system pressures. Their own priorities and psychology drive centralism. Power is seductive, and most ministers think they have been elected to take decisions, not to give their hard-won control away to someone else. This is particularly true shortly after an election, when a new administration wants to implement its manifesto. Incoming ministers often over-estimate what they can achieve in the short term and under-estimate their potential long-term impact. They start parliaments with high hopes for changing the world and only later realise the limits of their power. Recent history suggests that the way to make devolution happen is through a major push early in the life of a new government, and yet this is precisely the time when ministers are most likely to want to believe in the power of the centre.

The way Whitehall is structured does not help. Britain may be a very centralised country, but the civil service is quite the opposite, a decentralised world of baronies with surprisingly little coordination from the central triumvirate of Treasury, Downing Street and the Cabinet Office. Any programme of devolution requires a number of different departments to work together: the Treasury needs to be on board, but so too do the parts of government that are expected to devolve power, like the Health or Business departments. The Conservatives wanted to drive devolution, but they made the mistake of allowing each secretary of state to set his or her own policy direction when in opposition. This meant that, once in power, they struggled to establish a single strategic direction. Once they are in the hands of their new department, even the more radical type of minister is rapidly schooled in the long-established rules of the Whitehall game. The civil service is a deeply conservative force within British public life. This was most obvious when it came to the Big Society, a hugely ambitious idea that needed to be driven across almost every single government department but in practice received no substantial backing at all.

It may seem obvious that local politicians should back efforts to devolve power, but in reality this is not always the case. One of the key problems lies in deciding to which level power should be devolved. It makes very little sense for Wakefield to commission its own skills provision. People who live in the town often work and study outside of it, and travel to jobs across and beyond West Yorkshire. If you want to devolve power, you need councils to work together across boundaries. This is as true for skills provision as it is for transport, policing and fire services. While Greater Manchester has grasped the nettle and created a mayor for the whole conurbation, providing clear accountability for new devolved powers, many other parts of the country are very reluctant to take this step. Wakefield and Bradford are nervous about being overshadowed by Leeds; Sunderland does not want to play second fiddle to Newcastle. Local politicians face many of the same psychological barriers as their national counterparts – they seldom want to see their own role diminished or their organisation abolished even if that results in the devolution of power.

The general public usually need to give at least tacit approval to attempts to decentralise power but, perhaps unsurprisingly for a culture that has been so centralised for so long, the people are often slow to respond. Practical reforms such as free schools and neighbourhood planning have tended to fare reasonably well. More strategic attempts at democratic devolution – the kind that hands substantial new powers to a lower tier of government – have been less successful. When the government held referendums for US-style executive mayors in most of England's big cities in 2012, only Bristol voted in favour and turnout across the country was well under a third of eligible voters. It did not help that councillors in those cities were often vehemently opposed to the mayoral model and that the government refused to spell out the new powers that it would devolve if cities voted in favour. Cameron's only concrete pledge was a new 'cabinet of mayors' that he would chair. It turned out to be a very exclusive club. Later that year, the government held votes to elect new Police and Crime Commissioners, individuals who take over the governance of local police forces. Turnout was even worse, at just 15%, and was not helped by a lack of publicity and a polling date in the depths of a chilly November.

There are four broad ways to build an alliance for devolution. The first is for national politicians to reach over the heads of local elites and appeal directly to the people. This tends to lead to developments such as patients' choice of hospitals, or citizen-led initiatives in areas like planning. The second is for national politicians to make an alliance with local political elites, leading to initiatives such as the Greater Manchester mayor, in which devolution happens in the face of local indifference. The third alliance is between local elites and the people. This is rare in British history, but we can see an example in the Scottish independence referendum, in which the Scottish National Party (SNP) had sufficient public support to force the issue, against Westminster's wishes.

The final, and most effective, way to make democratic devolution work is to try to engage all three parties in the same discussion, aligning national politics, local elites and the people themselves. This approach underpinned the two biggest successes of the past 30 years: Scotland's parliament and London's mayoralty. They prove that the politicians' mend-and-make-do approach to the British constitution can be overcome.

2 How Scotland and London won their freedom

The first time a British government tried to devolve power to Scotland, it proved a spectacular failure. Pressure for devolution had been building since the 1960s as deindustrialisation and the end of empire forced the Scots to reconsider their position in the world. The SNP had begun to emerge as a serious electoral force and its call for independence was significantly bolstered by the discovery of North Sea oil, which created the potential for a country that might become economically self-sufficient. In response, Edward Heath declared his support for the idea of devolution and Harold Wilson set up a commission to examine the constitution of Britain. It reported in 1973 in favour of a Scottish Parliament, but, in a sign of things to come, the commission's verdict was not unanimous.[5]

There was nothing at all aligned about this attempt to give power away. The plans for a devolved assembly were cooked up in London, and Labour's Scottish executive committee voted against the proposals by six to five. The policy was saved only by another vote at the national Labour Party conference. The idea did not feature in the party's February 1974 general election manifesto, but it was included in the party's platform by the time of the election held in October of that year.[6] A first stab at legislation failed to pass through the House of Commons in 1977, only to be brought back onto the agenda when Jim Callaghan signed a deal with the Liberals to prop up his ailing Labour administration.

The Bill faced a rough ride from Unionists in Parliament, and by the time it passed, the legislation required a referendum before it could be put into effect, and that the 'Yes' side must be supported by at least 40% of eligible voters. The campaign for a 'Yes' vote was fragmented and lacklustre. An attempt to create an official cross-party grouping failed, with the result that Labour, the SNP and the Liberals ran separate campaigns. This was a campaign that offered voters a bewildering array of different messages, compared to the simplicity offered by the 'No' side. In the final event, the 'Yes' side won the slimmest of majorities but failed to meet the 40% threshold. The whole thing was a mess: conceived in Westminster, highly politicised, with no real agreement about the level of power that should be devolved. National politicians who did not quite believe in devolution had made an unconvincing offer to a country that was still making its mind up. Unsurprisingly, the whole shaky project fell, and so, too, did Callaghan.

Yet, far from killing off the idea of devolution, the 1979 referendum became the starting point for a very different approach to change. The underlying issues that fuelled Scottish nationalism had not gone away and the country's increasing cultural confidence combined with its profound alienation from the Thatcher governments to promote an ongoing debate about its future. The first principle for many devolution campaigners was that this time the planning should be led from Scotland rather than Westminster. By 1989 the Scottish Constitutional Convention had emerged as the leading voice on the issue. It could not command the support of the SNP, which refused to participate because independence was not being discussed. The Tories did not take part either. It was, nonetheless, a broadly based grouping that brought together trade unions, councils, small businesses and the Church to produce a series of reports on the future of the country.

While the Scots were busily securing buy-in from their countrymen and their own political elites, the Labour Party remained committed to introducing devolution once it was returned to power. Several key figures in the high command were very committed to a Scottish Parliament. Tony Blair was not a convinced devolutionary, but came to see the creation of a new assembly as inevitable. When his government called a Scottish referendum in 1997, the result was a resounding 'Yes' vote of almost 75%.

Of course, this was only the beginning of the story. The new Parliament rapidly cemented itself into the British constitution because it provided clear local accountability for the services Scotland used. Whereas in England the public tend to default to Westminster when there is a problem, the Scots blame their own Parliament for things like rising waiting lists and falling exam results.[7] The spiral of centralism had been broken. The danger now is that it has been broken to such an extent that the residual connection of the Scottish people to the Westminster Parliament is slowly fading. The SNP and its supporters in civil society appear to have learned the lesson of 1997, building a vibrant and energetic coalition of the political elite and 45% of the population in favour of independence. By contrast, the disastrous 'Better Together' campaign appeared to be taking all of its lessons from the 1979 campaign, refusing until the very last minute to make a unified cross-party offer of more devolution to the people of Scotland.

The Scottish settlement of 1997 left some awkward questions unanswered, and the surprisingly close result of the 2014 referendum campaign has brought them back onto the agenda. How can we justify the fact that Scotland receives more public money per head of population than Wales and the English regions? How do we justify the right of Scottish MPs to vote on English legislation? Have the English themselves reached a stable sense of their own identity and a consensus about their own future governance?

London's experience might provide some answers to that last question. Margaret Thatcher's decision to abolish the GLC in 1986 was widely seen as a partisan move to put a stop to Ken Livingstone's high-profile campaigning against her government. At one point, the leader of the GLC installed a gigantic banner that displayed unemployment statistics on the front of his headquarters, which happened to be directly across the river from Parliament. But for all the provocation that he offered to Thatcher, it is hard to see how the abolition of the GLC can possibly have been designed to lead to better administration. The UK's capital became the only major world city without a strategic local authority, and functions such as transport were hived off to unaccountable boards and quangos. The GLC was far from perfect, but its abolition created many more problems than it solved.

Labour's policy in the late 1980s was effectively to recreate the GLC, but, over time, attitudes started to change. Central government started to coordinate its own work far more effectively, creating a regional office and a dedicated minister for the city. The 32 boroughs also started to coordinate their own work far more effectively, working across boundaries in areas such as transport. They would eventually signal their assent to a new pan-London authority in 1996. The idea of recreating a big new bureaucracy to run swathes of public services started to fade. At the same time, the idea of introducing US-style city mayors in the UK entered the debate. It had been promoted by both Michael Heseltine and the journalist Simon Jenkins, who chaired a major commission on local democracy in the mid-1990s. It found a warm welcome in the bosom of the Yankophile Tony Blair and his inner circle. Despite some ructions within the party – the old guard led by shadow Environment Secretary Frank Dobson wanted something more like a traditional county council – the idea of a London mayor became policy.[8]

Translating the mayoralty into practice would prove tricky. Dobson's opposition to the idea saw him moved out of the way, into the Department of Health. Some in central government lobbied very hard to hang on to powers such as the appointment of the Metropolitan Police Commissioner. What emerged was a peculiarly British institution: a powerful executive mayor who actually did not run all that much. London's mayoralty was initially designed to chair boards, set strategies and sometimes make appointments to a wide range of bodies, including Transport for London and the Metropolitan Police Authority (which holds the capital's police force to account). This set-up could command enough support from national politicians to keep the relevant departments on board, while most local politicians recognised the need for a city of what was then seven million people to have some sort of strategic government. The fact that the new Greater London Authority (GLA) would have only very limited control over the boroughs' powers helped – excepting their strategic planning powers, the mayor would not initially challenge local government vested interests in substantial ways, although that would change over time. Now all that remained was the people.

The referendum that set up the GLA would prove to be a disappointment. Although the vote was won in every borough, including notoriously recalcitrant Bromley, only a third of voters bothered to turn out, perhaps reflecting a sense that the result was a foregone conclusion. Three-quarters of those who did vote said 'yes'. The election campaign that followed proved to be even more dispiriting as Labour struggled to block Ken Livingstone from winning the mayoralty, twisting the arm of a hapless and increasingly miserable Frank Dobson to stand in a rigged process to become the official Labour candidate. It was hardly better for the Conservatives, who lost their front runner due to a perjury charge.

But once the mayor was in place, the benefits became clear. Despite his limited formal powers, Livingstone proved adept at using his profile and mandate to get things done. It is impossible to imagine that the London congestion charge would have happened without the mayoralty. The Crossrail project to link Reading, in the west, to Shenfield, in Essex, was discussed for at least 20 years before London's mayor made it happen. The office has twice received new powers. Londoners are now far more likely to blame the mayor for poor-quality public transport than they are to blame

Westminster, although the same is not true of policing, where the mayor's powers and accountability have not always been so clear. The cycle of centralism has been at least partially broken, but there is further to go. London's sheer scale gives the mayor huge heft – Transport for London's revenue budget is much larger than the Department of Transport's – but in international comparison the office is fairly weak, with New York's mayor, for instance, controlling about five times the funding of Boris Johnson.

What can we learn from these exercises in devolution? The first lesson is about the importance of clearly framing the problem and laying the groundwork. While neither the Scottish Parliament nor the London mayor went through unopposed, both initiatives solved what were perceived to be real governance problems for recognisable places. Scotland wanted more control over its own affairs. London needed city-wide coordination and leadership. These facts were widely understood by the public, they had been widely debated and considerable thought had gone into the solution for each problem over a number of years before power was actually devolved.

The second lesson is about the need to transfer really substantial powers: both Scotland and London took on major new areas of responsibility. The public are unlikely to back devolution when they do not think it is offering them anything new. This is a key lesson from the 2012 mayoral referendums, where voters were asked to change the way their council was run, but with no clear sense of what kind of devolution might follow. It is even truer of the failed 2004 referendum on regional government for the North-East, where the lack of substantial new powers allowed opponents to argue that the new assembly would become an expensive talking shop.

But if power is devolved without accountability, the spiral of centralism is likely to kick back in. Local people need to know who to complain to when things go wrong and, ultimately, who they can sack. Directly elected city bosses in the Bloomberg or Giuliani mould tend to have higher name recognition and to be viewed as providing stronger leadership.[9] Because of their profile and the connections they can build with media and on the national political scene, they are also very well placed to demand more power and money from Westminster, and to make trouble if they do not get it. Just look at what Boris Johnson and Ken Livingstone have achieved in London. That is why a reluctant Greater Manchester really does needs a mayor, and not just a committee of 10 council leaders.

3 An opportunity for change

When it is seen in this light, it is easy to understand why so few people accepted the invitation to join the government of Britain. David Cameron's administration offered a series of piecemeal and uncoordinated policies designed to devolve different powers in different ways. There was no sense of a coherent vision of a different society, nor of how that new society could possibly be created in practice. What did it mean for an ordinary resident of Sunderland to join the government of Britain? It meant that a citizen could help to save their local pub, or tweak the council's spatial plan. It did not mean that the same citizen could easily choose to spend more money on their local public services, or try to find ways to keep their local A&E department open. When campaigners in Lewisham defeated the Health Secretary in court over plans to scale back their nearest hospital, he simply promised to change the law so he could close their hospital, regardless.

The experiences of Scotland and London suggest that a different sort of conversation is necessary: one that stops offering the public penny-packets of power and instead gets to the heart of their disillusionment with politics and offers some clear solutions. Politicians tend to believe that the public are not interested in constitutional niceties, and they are right. But the public are interested in the future shape of government, the functioning of the public services that they use and the way in which political decisions play out in their everyday lives. At a time when basic services such as street cleaning are starting to creak under the weight of austerity, this kind of conversation is absolutely essential.

For the first time in a generation, it seems that real change might be possible. The first major policy act of the newly elected Conservative government was to proclaim the creation of a devolved Northern Powerhouse, with Greater Manchester-style powers handed to those cities that are prepared to adopt a mayor. The national and local political elites are starting to form an alliance. But Conservative devolution plans raise as many questions as they answer. Will George Osborne really devolve the financial powers that cities need to weather austerity, or is this just a way to blame local leaders for cuts? Can local leaders find a way to ensure that devolution revitalises local democracy and accountability, rather than just shifting power from an unaccountable national elite to the closed world of local party politics? Has the Chancellor created a space where a new progressive politics of power sharing can flourish, or is this all just a con?

If the public can be drawn into the debate, and given the starring role in shaping the future of their cities, then a new type of politics might still be possible.

SEVEN

Hack the state: how we can take power back

History will not overthrow national governments; it will outflank them. (Alexander Trocchi[1])

Putting people back at the heart of politics has the potential to transform the way that society works for the better. By unlocking the power that is caged in central governments and sharing it with the public, we can create a world in which democracy is about creativity and contribution, not just consumption, a place in which ordinary people are really in charge of the support they receive from the state, and where unsustainable public services are rescued by untapped reserves of people power. It is a place where the state spends more of its time creating good jobs and healthier people than on footing the bill for unemployment and sickness. It is a country that does not have to rely on the failed institutions of the big, central state because it possesses thousands of small institutions of the commons and the city that can defend the interests of communities against the demands of both government and business.

It is a place that passionately values social progress, but is deeply sceptical about the idea that statism can deliver it. It puts the idea of liberty at the heart of society, but recognises that liberty can flourish only when individuals are educated, economically secure and able to make a contribution to the common good. It is a place defined by that mix of democratic republicanism and libertarian socialism that we might now term *commonism*, a politics that is developing across the globe, from New York to Bologna, from Iceland to Albania and beyond.

Technology is making our experience of the world simultaneously more global and more local. We can connect and collaborate with people in Shanghai and San Francisco at a moment's notice, but at the same time we are starting to recognise that in a knowledge economy the most efficient forms of production happen across clusters of firms centred in great places. We need a politics that can embrace both of these ideas at once, valuing the local and specific while at the same time looking outwards to the ideas and resources of the wider world.

In the past, centralism was seen as an antidote to the narrow parochialism of the parish pump, but today the tables have decisively turned. Westminster politics has become inward-looking and it is cities like London, Manchester, Cardiff and Glasgow that embody outward-facing dynamism. The same trend can be discerned across the world: see how America's gridlocked federal government compares to the vibrancy of New York and Portland, Oregon, or how cities across southern Europe are innovating to deal with the austerity caused in part by the decisions of their national governments. How do we create a world in which a carnival of open, liberating localism can defeat the regimented greyness of a declining central state?

There is a chart I often use in presentations.[2] It shows a line rising, peaking, falling and then rising again, depicting two summits with a trough in between. The first summit is labelled 'peak state', and it represents the zenith of government's role in British national life. The idea is based on that of peak oil, which is not the point at which we run out of fossil fuels, but the point at which we pass our maximum ability to extract them from the ground. The fuel that government runs on is taxation. This is a renewable resource, but, even so, there is plenty of evidence to suggest that the state will increasingly struggle to raise very high levels of it. Even if it could, the money would quickly be soaked up by ever-rising demand for health and social care services, leaving everything else in a state of crisis. If we have not already passed peak state, then we are very close to it.

This is a scary conclusion, but we should not be fatalistic about it. Britain is fundamentally a stable country with a robust economy. It will take a lot more than a financial crisis and an austerity programme to blow us back to the crisis of the 1930s. Instead, we will find ways to adapt to a different world. New understandings and ways of relating to one another and to government will emerge over time. The question is whether we will achieve a new equilibrium by defaulting to cheap and nasty public services and simply shifting more of what used to be public spending into the private sector, or whether we can pioneer the kind of approach to government for the 21st century that is described in this book. If the first peak on my chart represents peak state, the second represents the new, commonist settlement that could and should eventually emerge from the current crisis.

In between the two peaks is a deep trough called 'the valley of nobody knows'. This is where the transition happens, where the old settlement still has a tight grip on our imaginations but the new is starting to be born. The valley is the really scary bit of the chart, because it is the part where we feel lost and confused, where some people lose and others win. We have been here before. The 1930s was arguably a valley of nobody knows. In that case, governments had to change radically to overcome the limitations of the gold standard and introduce new forms of Keynesian demand management, followed by the widespread introduction of welfare states across the developed world. The late 1970s was also a valley of nobody knows, in which Keynesian demand management itself became a barrier to modernising a crumbling industrial economy.

The good news is that what emerged from both of these valleys was a new settlement that supported a fresh wave of economic development. Indeed, some economists argue that the current crisis of government should really be viewed as a process of adapting our institutions to the challenges posed by a networked knowledge economy. If they are right, then skilfully navigating the valley of nobody knows is just a transitional stage to a new 'golden age' akin to the post-war boom, in which we fully integrate new technology into our economy and create a new way for society to progress.[3] It may take a while for our institutions to adapt: the first stirrings of the welfare state emerged from Bismarck's Germany in the 1890s but the settlement as we know it took half a century to become fully formed in Britain. And like the previous valleys, successfully emerging from this one requires us to abandon some big ideas that are no longer useful. This time, it is not the gold standard or Keynes that must be tackled, but the idea of centralism itself.

The problem of descending into the valley of nobody knows is that we do not know the way out. We do not know how to get from peak state to peak commonism, or we would be doing it already. This chapter offers a route map that can guide the lost and confused out of the mist and up from the valley floor to the sunlit uplands of a new relationship between citizen, state and business. It will not tell you precisely what we might find there, but it will show you where the path is and point you in the right direction.

There are three principles that we can use to guide us. The first is that change will not come from grand theoretical narratives. This is not a question of describing a utopian society and then setting out clear steps from here to there. The very nature of a decentralised world suggests that the method of travel is more important than the precise details of the destination. If we create a society in which people can take power for themselves and experiment with it, then the best ideas will emerge and grow and the rest will fall away. Something better will emerge fairly rapidly from thousands of small attempts at change. The challenge is to ensure that the state is open and porous so that it can be changed from without. We do not have time to waste in waiting for government to transform itself.

The second principle is that the idea of *policy* gets us only so far. You cannot build a democracy of doing with a few tweaks to incentives and funding streams. Even the more radical ideas set out below will not do the job on their own: that requires the public to want to participate, something that can come only from leadership, convening and deliberation. A government White Paper may be a good starting point, but in isolation it is likely to be worthless. The Labour Party was a popular movement before it became the machine that built the 1945 welfare state, and we may need a similar sort of movement to create its successor.

Third, we must be clear that this is not a call for a form of municipal anarchy. Instead, it is a world in which there is a much larger domain of self-organised activity, but the state still plays a critical role. There will still be a health service, but it will spend a lot more of its money on preventing illness, and consequently we will use it a lot less. We will know that we have succeeded when people start holding parties to mark the demolition of old hospital buildings that are no longer necessary. There will still be parks, libraries and green spaces, but they may be owned by communities, and some of them may even generate a surplus to reinvest in local commons. There will still be learning and skills, though they may increasingly be delivered by peer-to-peer action. In a country as unequal as Britain we will always need the state as the final guarantor of fairness.

1 New roles for nation states

The first thing we need to do is describe a new strategic role for central government. Where should Whitehall and Westminster lead, and when should they get out of the way? Leaving aside naturally centralised functions such as defence and foreign policy, the simple answer is that as the central state reaches the limits of its ability to solve many of the problems created by society and the market, then it will need to find a new role in helping the other two estates to address their own challenges. In a more decentralised world, the key job for Westminster will be to put resources into the commons and keep a careful watch on what emerges at the other end, always with an eye to evening out inequalities. This means that government should step back from many of the service-delivery functions it performs today and instead focus on creating the conditions in which people can lead good lives, free from domination by others.

The most important of those macro conditions is a certain level of basic financial security. Without this, ordinary people cannot be said to be free, nor can they make a contribution to the commons. The best way to ensure this sort of security is to make sure that as many people as possible are able to access good jobs: one of central government's most important goals should be full employment. Ministers must take a lot more interest in the quality of work, investing heavily in learning and skills to produce a higher-quality workforce, while simultaneously putting public money into innovation, the adoption of new technology and the use of better management techniques to increase productivity. We will need some new policy interventions to help mothers find affordable, commons-based childcare and ensure that at least some new jobs are flexible enough to accommodate older workers and the disabled.

Of course, some of this will cost money, but it is a set of investments that bear a substantial return for the government in the form of increased tax revenues, reduced benefits payments and income from ongoing stakes in basic innovation.[4] On some calculations, introducing universal free childcare would generate a net return of slightly more than £20,000 to the government over four years for every woman who returned to full-time work after a year of maternity leave.[5] Many of these policies would become self-financing, ensuring that they did not lead to an ever-bigger central state.

Central government also needs to ensure that enough people have the time and energy to contribute to maintaining the commons. It is easy to think about social action as something people do voluntarily in their spare time, but in fact it is work and needs to be at least partially recognised as such. Part of the answer is to ensure that people can make careers in the commons by supporting the creation of social enterprises and cooperatives, but we could tap into a far wider pool of energy and effort if we worked towards the introduction of a basic citizen's income.

This is the idea that instead of maintaining a complicated tax and benefits system, the government should give everyone a fixed amount of money a year as a right of citizenship. It would essentially take the benefits bill and divide it up more or less equally across the population. The Citizen's Income Trust suggests that the 2012/13 bill, excluding housing and disability costs, could have been used to pay a basic income of £56.25 a week to those under 25, £71 for 25- to 64-year-olds and £142.70 a week to those aged 65 plus.[6] The scheme would have the great advantages of massively reducing the benefits bureaucracy, ending the benefits trap entirely by ensuring that people kept every extra penny they earned and ending extreme poverty. It would, however, require the abolition of the personal tax allowance and higher-rate tax relief on pension contributions.

The introduction of a basic income is not just a utopian pipe dream. It has been trialled on a small scale in Canada and parts of the developing world with some success. At the time of writing, the Dutch city of Utrecht was planning a pilot of basic income, and the Finnish government also appeared to be committed to testing the idea. One way or another, it seems very likely that a major nation will try this system in the foreseeable future. We will soon know more about how it works. However, it is clear that a British basic income would require a big shift in attitudes to welfare: as well as finding enough money to set a rate that could provide for more than quite basic subsistence, we would have to accept the idea that everyone received a minimum, regardless of their circumstances.[7] This might become much more palatable if inequality continued to rise and a new wave of automation hit society. If robots really can take on half the jobs in the economy, then we will need some new coping mechanisms to manage the implications. The logical conclusion of this process would be that the owners of capital would get a lot richer and ordinary people would get a lot poorer. A new balance might be found after a time as the economy generated new types of job, or it might not. The best-case scenario would probably be a difficult process of transition. Such a situation might help to justify the higher taxes needed to make a decent minimum income affordable. If a basic income had the effect of reducing wage costs, then it is reasonable that employers should pay a substantial share of those higher taxes.

A basic income cannot magic away social pathologies such as drug addiction and domestic violence. It cannot do away with the fact that some people will try to live on benefits without making a wider contribution to society, although a citizen's income would make benefit fraud pointless. There would still be reasons why some people did not work. However, for the vast majority of people, a guaranteed basic income would be a way to work less and create more time for childcare, keeping healthy, contributing to their neighbourhood and helping to secure the common good. Perhaps most importantly, a citizen's income would transform the benefits system from a means of controlling and punishing people into an engine for liberating them. Bad employers would find it harder to hang on to staff who knew their subsistence was guaranteed. Dysfunctional families would find it harder to keep abused partners or children at home. People with a guaranteed income would have more choices before them.

Finally, the central state needs to lead a different kind of conversation about the social role of business. This is not necessarily about finding clever new ways to tax companies, but about the way that corporations make a contribution to the places where they do business. We can already see examples of this sort of conversation in action at a local level. Enfield, in North London, has produced an analysis of the 20 largest companies providing goods and services in the area and has challenged them to reinvest more of their profit in the area. Tesco, for instance, makes around £8.1 million of profit from its local branches but its social contribution amounts to a community toilet scheme, some charity fundraising stalls and a schools and clubs programme. We need the central state to make a similar challenge to business at the national and international levels.

This should be accompanied by the development of new regulatory approaches that give business a longer-term stake in the investment decisions it makes. This has been termed a 'skin in the game' approach.[8] One application lies in the area of fracking. At present the government requires that companies should pay a small proportion of their profits to local residents to compensate them for the disruption. Under a skin-in-the-game approach, the amount the company paid might be tied to the impact of its activities on local house prices, which are a rough proxy for quality of life in the local area. This would force a fracking company to pay attention to the long-term impact of its activities. It is possible to imagine some very radical applications of this principle to public-private partnerships. For instance, a company that redeveloped a council estate might enter into a 30-year contract where it was paid according to whether or not social outcomes on the estate were improving. This would ensure that initial design decisions were taken with the long term in mind, and not just with an eye to immediate profit.[9]

What the central state should do far less of is social policy. As we have seen, much of this work can be devolved to cities and counties. We have already seen big chunks of the health and skills systems devolved to Greater Manchester, albeit within a framework of national accountability. There is no reason why a much wider range of services could not be devolved in a similar fashion, from probation and prisons to a greater say in the benefits system and direct control of certain aspects of that system, such as housing benefit. There is no reason, in principle, why a city mayor for Greater Bristol, West Yorkshire or Tyne and Wear could not wield most of the same functions that have been devolved to the Scottish government, and there are only a few functions that very obviously could not be localised. For instance, while many national taxes could be collected locally, some of the rates need to be set nationally. Full devolution of income and corporation taxes, for instance, would be likely to lead to a damaging race to the bottom as cities competed to attract businesses and wealthy individuals by gutting each other's tax bases. A little of this sort of competition might be healthy, but too much would be disastrous.

We need to carefully consider the way in which this devolution would be managed. There is something oxymoronic about the idea of a national programme or constitutional convention for giving power away, especially as we need to engage the public much more fully in the discussion. Power should be pulled downwards by cities and counties at a pace that suits them. The obvious place to start would be with local constitutional conventions modelled on the Scottish experience. Local people, civil society and councils need to have a full debate about the future governance of their conurbations and counties and then draw down new powers. Each convention would then send delegates to a national constitutional convention that would frame a written constitution and set out the future role of the national level of government in a devolved world.

The only checks on the process should be the willingness of local people to accept devolution and the fact that power needs to be exercised at the right level in an accountable fashion. Salford should not be able to run its own version of the NHS, but the mayor of Greater Manchester would take on a lot more responsibility for commissioning primary care and reshaping the hospital sector. The need to convince local people about devolution proposals would act as a safeguard against poorly performing councils taking on more power than they could manage. Local people should have their say either through constitutional conventions or a formal referendum.

There is very little point in devolving more power unless cities also get more control of their own funding. Local government finance is a famously complex topic, but it is possible to see three clear principles that should underpin a new approach. The first is that central government should continue to redistribute money between cities, but that it should take the bare minimum necessary to ensure basic fairness. This might be as low as a third of the business rate. The second is that councils should be given a greater stake in the economic growth that they help to create, by capturing a greater share of rising wages and profits. The third principle is that incentives for growth should be balanced by incentives for sustainability. Councils should gain powers to tax carbon emissions through a combination of congestion-charging schemes and a licensing regime for heavier emitters. This would ensure that growth was driven in an environmentally sensitive way. Council tax would probably still be a part of a new system, but it would be a much smaller part of the overall funding mix and this would make large tax increases much less likely.

The end goal needs to be a system in which local people can express real democratic choices about the services they receive, not just choosing from a limited menu set in Whitehall but being engaged in a real debate about the future of healthcare and education in their city, and with easier ways to choose to pay more through the tax system if that is what they want. Putting power into the hands of cities would make these conversations easier. All of a sudden, the NHS would be not just about your local hospital or the future of a national system, but about the quality of care you can access across the city. Just as importantly, by putting more

control over the health service into the hands of local government
we could redesign healthcare around prevention and well-being,
and not just throw ever more money at expensive treatments. It
is far easier to cut through the complexity of all these choices at a
local level, where we can see real people and services for what they
are and not just as abstract numbers on a Whitehall spreadsheet.

2 Turning public services into commons

Governments change very slowly, even if it does not always look
that way. The febrile restructuring of departments and institutions
often makes it appear that everything is being transformed all the
time, but the truth is that the underlying behaviour and values
of public sector organisations are incredibly resilient. All the
restructuring is generally just a way to make up for the limited
power that the central state really has to change the world. The
problem we face today is that we need the underlying behaviour
of our institutions to change very quickly indeed. The only option
is to encourage a very polite, but very firm, insurrection. We need
people to come in from outside the traditional public sector and
hack the state, finding ways to implement new technology and
develop new services without having to move at the pace of
official notices and public procurement procedures. The state needs
to find ways to support the people who will rip up and remake
government.

   The first step is to start investing in creating a sense of social
possibility in places. Edi Rama used paint to convince the people
of Tirana that something could be done to improve their city.
Across Britain, people are achieving something similar by growing
their own food. The Yorkshire town of Todmorden, for instance,
has benefited from a programme to grow fruit and vegetables in
public places, with people being encouraged to pick and eat it
for free. Councils should start encouraging local people to take
over waste ground, verges and front gardens to create impromptu
allotments, growing fruit and vegetables that anyone can pick; to
create more social capital, grow food everywhere and create a
shared resource in which everyone has a stake. If local people ever

asked a councillor "what is the commons?", the politician could simply offer them an apple from a nearby tree.

We need to stop focusing so closely on the size of government, as if the potential for social progress can be measured solely by the proportion of GDP that we spend on the state. It is not just money that matters, but whether that money is spent on the right things and whether it helps to create the right conditions for the commons to emerge. So instead of focusing on the proportion of GDP controlled by the state, we need a new measure that we might call *total social resource*, or TSR, which can capture the full range of resources going into achieving social outcomes from all sources. This would include assets, time, donations and contributions from business. If the size of government shrinks a little, but the size of TSR rises significantly to compensate, then that is probably OK. A smaller state is nothing to fear if we also have a smaller private sector and the gap is filled with social energy. Measuring TSR would place pressure on governments, locally and centrally, to maximise the resources available to the commons.

As local authorities took on much more power, they would need to open up their services radically to allow others to innovate and experiment in ways that maximised the commons. This would mean creating new ways of funding and commissioning that put an end to monolithic public service provision and instead allowed a thriving undergrowth of social businesses to innovate and transform the way we support people.[10] British public services could learn a huge amount from Cincinnati's StriveTogether about how to align the state's work with lots of smaller not-for-profits. The first thing we need is a way to grow an ecosystem of social enterprises, which currently does not exist in many British cities. Then we need some form of public sector commissioning hub that can ensure that social enterprises are stringently evaluated and are paid for the results they deliver. The new system would need to be jointly governed by the state, citizens, businesses and the social enterprises themselves to ensure that it delivered on the biggest challenges facing any given city.

We should grow our base of innovative social enterprises through the creation of a new network of city-level social foundations.

Britain has a National Endowment for Science, Technology and the Arts, now we need Local Foundations for the Commons (LFC). Each foundation would be capitalised partly by money from central government, or through borrowing from national social finance organisations such as Big Society Capital. The government's shares in the nationalised banks might also be vested in the local foundations as a long-term investment in their success. There would also be local money, perhaps from a 1% tariff on every public procurement made in the city, plus contributions from private individuals and businesses.[11] The local foundations would be governed by a mix of donors, grantees and local people, who would work with public service leaders to develop a shared investment agenda. Their purpose would be to incubate and evaluate new approaches to service delivery up to the point where they could start to receive public funding. Their only mandatory legal goal might be to maximise the total social resource of the place they served.

The next step would be for councils and other parts of the public sector to move away from their traditional approach of achieving social outcomes through in-house service delivery or big block contracts to the private sector, and instead to introduce a licensing regime to allow a far wider range of smaller organisations to get involved. A local authority might identify a small number of priority outcomes across its city – for instance, increasing health and well-being or reducing unemployment. It would then create a commissioning hub, aligned with the investment plans of the local foundation, that would set out an evidence-based route map describing what the goal meant in practical terms and how it could be achieved, drawing on high-quality data and ensuring regular cycles of evaluation to see where its approach was working.

The commissioning hub would then create a pricing structure setting out how much it would offer organisations for helping to achieve, for instance, reductions in levels of diabetes and loneliness, or increases in the capacity of people to manage their own medical conditions. The commissioners would also create a licensing regime. Anyone could apply for a licence as long as they met its conditions, which might include professional certification, minimum levels of insurance and conditions around social responsibility. As far as possible, the licensing regime should favour small, innovative and employee- or community-owned organisations. Ultimately, the local foundations in particular should aim to support organisations that helped to grow and maintain civic commons, giving local people ownership of assets and a voice in the way services were managed.

So, for instance, Greater Manchester might decide that its key goal was to reduce pressure on the NHS by promoting wellness across the city. The conurbation's mayor would ensure that discussions took place with the LFC and its partners about creating an investment programme to support organisations that would promote preventative health. Then the city's councils would work with the health service to create a joint commissioning hub that would examine the best available evidence and create a route map for the kinds of interventions that would be likely to improve well-being. The hub would create a pricing structure showing how organisations could earn payments for contributing towards Greater Manchester's well-being, and a licensing system setting minimum standards for participation.

All the public sector players involved would need to commit to opening up their data to allow potential new entrants to spot gaps in the market and to inspire the creation of new technological tools that could help to promote well-being. The hub would also want to keep a close watch on the TSR it was mobilising, perhaps requiring a certain amount of social 'match funding' for every investment it made. The combination of capital investment from the LFC for early-stage development with outcome payments and a public regulatory regime would allow a wide range of new players to enter the market. It would provide a way to rapidly grow organisations that contributed to the commons by creating shared assets and putting citizens in charge of the way services were delivered.

This would not represent the privatisation or weakening of local authorities, or indeed of any other public services. Local authorities that took on significantly more power from Whitehall would still have a wide range of strategic functions to manage, from shaping the local economy to strategic health commissioning, and they would retain the power to set outcomes and licensing conditions for the commons. The built-in preference for commons-based solutions, the focus on TSR and the lack of big up-front contracts would deter the private sector from hijacking the system.

There are two further reforms that councils need to make in order to grow the commons. The first is a new wave of initiatives to bring the young and the old back into the commons-based workforce. Unemployed young people need to be able to access support to set up their own social enterprises, with some start-up funding and a business adviser. This would provide them with extraordinarily valuable workplace experience as well as contributing to the commons in a particular place. Over time, this could become a sort of 'social gap year' after school or university. New schemes must also be developed to bring older people back into the social workforce, helping them to find clear roles in retirement through schemes like surrogate grandparenting, or mainstream volunteering to maintain commons such as parks, libraries or community centres. The baby boomer generation currently hitting retirement age is, in aggregate, the best-educated, healthiest and wealthiest cohort in history. We must make sure that we capitalise on this extraordinary reserve of skills and energy.

The second is the radical democratisation of local government's customer-contact functions. At present, I might call the council (usually reluctantly) to pay a bill or file a complaint. Over the coming years, the internet will render this sort of interaction completely unnecessary. I do not need to call the council to pay my council tax if it has a decent website. Moving to digital public services has the potential to put the local authority call centre out of business. Instead of doing that, we need to move to a new model of customer contact in which the call centre is not directing me to someone who can help, but linking me to ways in which I can help myself and others.

If I call the council today to discuss my elderly neighbour, the chances are that I will be funnelled towards a social worker. In future, I may be offered training to support the neighbour myself, or details of a nearby social enterprise that can help.

Council customer contact centres should be mutualised, spun off and radically decentralised, with their support functions turned into simple apps that are then distributed to the owners of hair salons, post offices and pubs. If I want to contact a local public service or find social support, I should take a trip to the pub and ask the proprietor to help me find the right support on her iPad over a drink, while they receive a small payment every time they successfully resolve a contact. This would help to build trust and civic infrastructure, while simultaneously providing a revenue stream for valued community assets.

3 Radically open politics

British politics is stuck in a rut. The great leaders of the British experiment with centralism – the Attlees, Thatchers and Blairs – have very little to teach us about leading in the age of the network, and yet they remain touchstones for many contemporary politicians. Glimmers of something new can be seen emerging from the shattered economies of continental Europe, from the sophisticated policy crowdsourcing of the German Pirate Party to the online phenomenon of Beppe Grillo's Five Star movement, which transformed itself from an internet phenomenon into the largest party in the Italian Parliament during a single election. But these are best understood as experiments. The internet makes it easy to mobilise bursts of rage, and it can be used for longer-run deliberation, but it cannot substitute for the discipline and coherence necessary to gain a secure foothold from which to transform establishment politics.

Quieter, local experiments may be driving more lasting change. When Jon Gnarr's Best Party emerged as the largest group on Reykjavik's council, it used an online platform to inform its negotiating stance during coalition negotiations, a period during which 40% of the city's voters used the platform and 2,000 ideas were contributed. Eventually, the city council committed to considering the 10–15 ideas with the most votes on the site every month and responding to them, whether they were implemented or not.[12] Athens has launched a similar experiment with its

SynAthina platform. It is too early to describe what a new version of democracy for the networked age might look like, but we know that it will have to blend the traditional representative version with online participation and the emergence of the democracy of doing. It will involve ending the politicians' monopoly on decision making and sharing their power throughout society.

What links the Italian Parliament with Reykjavik city hall, and indeed with the parliaments of Greece and Spain, is the fact that new leadership often emerges from moments of convulsive crisis. These can comprehensively discredit existing elites and allow radically different kinds of leadership to come to the fore. The problem with change by crisis is that it can be very unpredictable. The Wall Street Crash and the Great Depression of the 1930s certainly shook the status quo across the globe. In the US, it created the conditions for Franklin Roosevelt's radically optimistic New Deal, but in Germany the same global forces played a role in bringing something much darker to the fore.

What we need in Britain is not a pregnant crisis but a controlled explosion. Of course, you could argue that this is already starting to happen: the two-party consensus has been crumbling for a generation. Generational change is starting to create a group of MPs and councillors who are much more comfortable with a world of online openness. But the networked society is still fighting a pitched battle against the forces of political party loyalty and group cohesion. Too many politicians use Twitter to broadcast their party messages or argue with their opponents; too few of them use it as a tool to inform their decision making. This may change as the next generation starts to take political office, but we must never underestimate the grip of party political culture and its ability to limit change. The key to allowing something new to emerge is to loosen the grip of mainstream politics and allow new leaders to emerge who are willing to share power.

It is easy to call for behavioural change on the part of political parties. Of course they should enthusiastically adopt innovations such as e-democracy, open primaries for selecting MPs and a much more open approach to selecting candidates from beyond traditional party structures. But the pace of change is infuriatingly slow because there is no real incentive for larger parties to innovate: why bother to change when you can stay the same and remain in power? If we want to force the pace, then we need to find a way to disrupt the system. If we want to engage the public in politics, then we should literally leave it to chance: allow ordinary people to become decision makers by selecting more of our politicians by lottery.

This approach underpinned Athenian democracy. For the ancient Greeks, elections were used to select oligarchies of the best and brightest, while the people were best represented by random selection. Sortition (drawing of lots) offers a way to radically broaden political engagement while working against the creation of a professional political elite and making it far harder for vested interests to capture the legislators. We recognise all of these qualities in the lotteries that are used to select more than 400,000 people a year to serve on juries. Why not do the same for at least some of our political institutions? Sortition should not completely replace elections but, rather, complement them. There is a strong argument that our prime ministers and home secretaries should be the best and brightest, that they need a decent spell in office in order to make a difference and that they should be held directly accountable by election. The role of lotteries should be in selecting people to deliberate and challenge.

The right place to start is with the House of Lords. There is cross-party agreement about the need to reform the wholly undemocratic upper chamber but no clear sense of what that reform should look like. The Lords should be turned into a new People's Chamber, with any willing citizen allowed to opt in to the ballot for a three-year term as a senator, backed by legislation to minimise the impact this might have on an individual's income and career prospects. Coupled with suitable training this would allow people from all walks of life to become leaders for a short period of time, and the ballot could be designed to ensure that the senators were genuinely representative of wider society in terms of the number of women and minorities represented. The best senators might go on to seek elected office. Sortition would solve a number of problems that have long vexed Lords' reformers. A new People's Chamber would not have the power to challenge the primacy of the House of Commons. Instead, like the existing House of Lords, it would have enough power to ensure that MPs had to take its views into account, but not so much that it could consistently block the will of the elected chamber. It would not build in an advantage for any given party, because its members would be randomly selected. But it would allow a far wider range of citizens to make their views heard.

Of course, in the world I am describing local leaders will be a lot more important than they are today: we need to pay equal attention to ensuring that a new politics emerges in our cities. In the same way that the new People's Chamber would scrutinise national policy, cities should create new mechanisms to allow randomly selected groups to examine key local decisions. Cities should set up local equivalents of the People's Chamber, supported by a professional group of officials, with the power to scrutinise any aspect of public policy, and its members selected by sortition for one-year terms. More radically, we could reduce the number of elected councillors by 25% across the country and replace them with members selected by lot for one-year terms. The new sortitioners would not be able to hold executive positions, but would otherwise enjoy the same rights as any other councillor. They would bring the voice of the ordinary man or woman into the council chamber, challenging the behaviour and culture of existing political parties and driving them in a more open and democratic direction. This would help to reduce the number of councils that were dominated by a single party and force many ruling groups to convince the sortitioners before taking decisions, arguably leading to a more consensual and democratic style of political leadership.

One of the ideas that Michael Young failed to sneak into the 1945 Labour manifesto[13] was that there should be an empty seat at the cabinet table in Downing Street to remind ministers of whom they were there to serve. The idea was a good one, but it might have seemed a lot less symbolic if he had proposed that the seat should actually be filled from time to time.

4 Towards a bigger 'us'

We live at a time of crisis and opportunity. It is a time when people are looking for someone to blame. For the Left, it is the bankers. For the Right, it is immigrants and welfare cheats. But the truth is that our challenges are systemic. It is not that the materials out of which our politicians are made have somehow become cheap and flammable, nor is it that some mysterious outside force is sapping our cultural energy. The problem is that society is changing, rapidly and dramatically, as technology reshapes the ways we interact with each other, provides metaphors for new forms of decentralised organisation and puts ever more power and capability into the hands of the individual. The twin challenges of technological progress and environmental brakes on growth are starting to point in the direction of a very different kind of economy and society. We should not be surprised that a centralised form of parliamentary democracy with its roots in the 17th century is struggling to keep up, nor that the stewards of that system have responded to the challenge of the networked age by retreating into a hyperreal media bubble, far removed from most people's everyday lives.

Centralism has been both a response to the decline of British political power and a cause of that decline. I have tried to demonstrate that any imaginable response to our current crisis of political legitimacy must start by letting go of the failed top-down politics of the past. We must begin the process of creating a freer society in which power is not locked up in 19th-century palaces on the Thames, but is shared by each and every one of us. This book has focused primarily on the challenge of state power, and particularly on social policy, but the same trends that are driving change in government are also working on the business world, forcing many companies to consider their social value and to search for new ways to reduce their overhead costs and devolve far more meaningful power to the front line. This is not a world without risks – big bureaucracies promised people security in return for obedience, while decentralisation can unlock creativity and dynamism at the cost of uncertainty. Which of these bargains do you think is more in keeping with the spirit of the age?

Ultimately, the way to ensure that we emerge into the 2020s as a stronger nation is not to draw more dividing lines between 'them' and 'us', but to radically expand our sense of what 'us' means, and then to rediscover what we can achieve together.

Notes

One: The revolution will not be centralised: why top-down politics won't survive the 21st century

[1] Blair, T. (2010) 'The importance of governance in the modern world', speech, Institute for Government.

[2] Tawney, R.H. (1920) *The acquisitive society*, New York: Harcourt, Brace and Company .

[3] Bakunin, M. (1867/1981) 'Federalism, socialism, anti-theologism' in S. Dolgoff (ed) *Bakunin on Anarchism*, Montreal.

[4] Carswell, D. (2011) 'Politics will be dominated by those with ideas to disperse power', available at http://www.talkcarswell.com/home/politics-will-be-dominated-by-those-with-ideas/2021.

[5] Jenkins, S. (2004) *Big bang localism: A rescue plan for British democracy*, London: Policy Exchange.

[6] OECD (2013) *Government at a glance*, Paris: OECD, p. 73.

[7] Clark, G. (2012) *Decentralisation: An assessment of progress*, London: DCLG .

[8] Thomas, B., Dorling, D. et al (2010) 'Inequalities in premature mortality in Britain: observational study from 1921 to 2007', *British Medical Journal*, vol 341: c3639.

[9] King, A. and Crewe, I. (2013) *The blunders of our governments*, UK: Oneworld Publications.

[10] Natcen Social Research, *British Social Attitudes: 31st edition*, Greater Britain: Natcen.

[11] Castells, M. (2009) *Communication power*, Oxford and New York: Oxford University Press.

[12] Parker, S. and Hallsworth, M. (2010) *What makes a 'successful' policy?*, London: Institute for Government.

[13] Heimans, J. and Timms, H. (2014) 'Understanding new power', *Harvard Business Review*, available at https://hbr.org/2014/12/understanding-new-power.

[14] Ilich, I. (1971) *Deschooling society*, New York: Harper and Row.

[15] Rushe, D. (2014) 'Is Uber the worst company in Silicon Valley?', *Guardian*, available at http://www.theguardian.com/technology/2014/nov/18/uber-worst-company-silicon-valley, accessed on 13 March 2015.

[16] See, for instance, McGovern, A. (2015) 'Labour's unfinished business: the children still living in poverty', *New Statesman*, available at http://www.newstatesman.com/politics/2015/02/labours-unfinished-business-children-still-living-poverty.

[17] DWP/DfE (2012) *Child poverty in the UK: The report on the 2010 target*, London: The Stationery Office.

[18] Case study based on Cristina Caballero, M. (2004) 'Academic turns city into a social experiment', *Harvard University Gazette*, available at http://news.harvard.edu/gazette/2004/03.11/01-mockus.html, and Dalsgard, A. (director) (2012) 'Improving civic behaviour – cities on speed', available at https://www.youtube.com/watch?v=bwgWM3h_l-4, accessed on 13 March 2015.

[19] See, for instance, Wilson, J. (2012) *Letting go*, UK: Fabian Society.

[20] Morris was a hero to both Tawney (who was an extremely close friend to Beveridge and married his sister) and G.D.H. Cole, both important inter-war Labour thinkers. Tony Crosland was among those who would call for a return to the William Morris tradition in the 1950s. A 2015 National Portrait Gallery exhibition highlighted the relevance of Morris's mix of craft, creativity and decentralisation to today's creative economy.

[21] Morris, W. (1908) *News from nowhere*, London: Longmans.

[22] Saatchi, M. (2014) *The road from serfdom*, London: Centre for Policy Studies.

[23] Solnit, R. (2009) *A paradise built in hell: The extraordinary communities that arise in disaster*, US: Penguin.

[24] Co-operatives UK (2014) 'The UK Co-operative economy 2014', available at http://www.uk.coop/resources/uk-co-operative-economy-2014-untold-resilience.

[25] Matheson, G. (2014) 'Speech by Councillor Gordon Matheson', available at https://www.glasgow.gov.uk/index.aspx?articleid=14319, accessed on 13 March 2015.

[26] Although it should be noted that the Webbs themselves were great supporters of local government, believing that there were compelling reasons why many functions should be municipalised rather than nationalised.

[27] See, for instance, Skinner, Q. (1997) *Liberty before liberalism*, Cambridge: Cambridge University Press, and Pettit, P. (1997) *Republicanism*, Oxford: Oxford University Press.

Two: Learning to love the postcode lottery: why hoarding power usually fails

[1] Google's Ngram viewer shows a small increase in mentions of the term 'postcode lottery' around 1980, followed by a rapidly growing number of mentions from 1995 onwards.

[2] Prince, R. (2011) 'Eric Pickles: public will lose faith in councils which fail to collect bins', *Daily Telegraph*, available at http://www.telegraph.co.uk/news/politics/conservative/8283779/Eric-Pickles-public-will-lose-faith-in-councils-which-fail-to-collect-bins.html, accessed on 16 March 15.

[3] Chapman, J. (2015) 'Tough talk on bins exposed as rubbish after NO councils sign up to £250million fund to restore weekly collections', *Daily Mail*, available at http://www.dailymail.co.uk/news/article-2908907/Pickles-bins-collection-fund-weekly-rounds-used-zero-councils-authority-considered-decided-expensive.html.

[4] Royal College of Surgeons (2014) 'Is access to surgery a postcode lottery?', available at: http://www.rcseng.ac.uk/news/docs/Is%20access%20to%20surgery%20a%20postcode%20lottery.pdf.

[5] See, for instance, Walker, D. (2002) 'Hold the centre', *Guardian*, available at http://www.theguardian.com/politics/2002/nov/21/budget2003.society.

[6] Townsend, E. (2009) *UK income inequality and international comparisons*, London: House of Commons Library, p 39.

[7] OECD (2010) 'A family affair: intergenerational social mobility across OECD countries', *Going for Growth*, Paris: OECD, p 185.

[8] See, for instance, NHS England (2013a) 'High quality care for all, now and for future generations', available at http://www.england.nhs.uk/wp-content/uploads/2013/06/urg-emerg-care-ev-bse.pdf.

[9] NLGN review of National Audit Office reports for this book.

[10] Parker, S., Paun, A. et al (2010) *State of the service*, London: Institute for Government .

[11] Freeguard, G., Munro, R. et al (2015) *Whitehall monitor: Deep impact?*, London: Institute for Government.

[12] Tomaney, J., Pike, A. et al (2011) *Decentralisation outcomes: A review of evidence and analysis of international data*, London: DCLG.

[13] Blöchliger, H. (2013) 'Decentralisation and Economic Growth – Part 1: How fiscal federalism affects long-term development', *OECD Working Papers on Fiscal Federalism*, No 14, OECD Publishing.

[14] City Growth Commission (2014) *Unlocking metro growth*, London: RSA.

[15] Ipsos MORI (2013) 'Leader perceptions poll', available at https://www.ipsos-mori.com/Assets/Docs/Polls/LeadershipPoll_topline.PDF.

[16] Blunkett, D. (2002) 'Responsibility without power: the worst of all worlds', excerpts available at: http://www.theguardian.com/society/2002/feb/01/publicservices, accessed on 3 April 15.

[17] Ipsos MORI (2010a) *What do people want, need and expect from public services?*, London: RSA.

[18] Powell, H. (2013) 'Local engagement and raising public confidence – what do the public think?', available at https://www.ipsos-mori.com/Assets/Docs/News/helen-powell-pcc-conference-policing-2013.pdf.

[19] See, for instance, Taylor-Gooby, P. (2006) '*The efficiency trust dilemma'*, working paper, ESRC SCARR Network: Canterbury.

[20] NHS England (2013b) 'The NHS belongs to the people: a call to action', available at www.england.nhs.uk/wp-content/uploads/2013/07/nhs_belongs.pdf.

[21] Monitor (2013) 'Closing the NHS funding gap: how to get better value healthcare for patients', available at https://www.gov.uk/government/uploads/system/uploads/attachment_data/file/284044/ClosingTheGap091013.pdf.

[22] Wanless, D. (2002) *Securing our future health: Taking a long term view*, UK: Her Majesty's Treasury.

[23] APPG on Primary Care and Public Health (2012) 'Ten years on from Wanless, how "fully engaged" are we?', available at http://www.pagb.co.uk/appg/inquiryreports/WanlessReview10yearson_2012.pdf.

[24] Marmot, M. (2014) Foreword, in *If you could do one thing*, London: British Academy.

[25] NHS England (2013b).

[26] NHS England (2014) 'Get serious about obesity or bankrupt the NHS', available at http://www.england.nhs.uk/2014/09/17/serious-about-obesity/.

[27] Greer, S. (2010) 'Options and the lack of options: healthcare politics and policy', in V. Uberoi et al (eds) *Options for Britain II*, UK: Wiley-Blackwell.

[28] Bullock, S. (2014) 'Local government and the NHS', in E. Burnell (ed), *Labour's local offer*, London: NLGN.

[29] Municipal Dreams blog: https://municipaldreams.wordpress.com/2014/03/04/the-hulme-crescents-manchester-bringing-a-touch-of-eighteenth-century-grace-and-dignity-to-municipal-building/.

[30] The documentary is no longer available on the BBC website, but you can get a sense of the Crescents' nostalgia from this article in the Municipal Dreams blog (2014): http://www.vice.com/en_uk/read/hulme-manchester-history-party-squats-109.

[31] See, for instance, Office of National Statistics (2009) 'Housing', in *Social Trends 39*, Houndmills: Palgrave Macmillan, chapter 10.

[32] Heath, S. (2014) *Housing demand and need (England)*, London: House of Commons Library.

[33] This data is ably summarised at https://fullfact.org/factchecks/house_building_housing_benefit-29316.

[34] Symons. T. and Rodriguez, L. (2011) *Build to let*, London: NLGN.

[35] Projections from Oxford Economics.

[36] Bivand, P. and Simmons, D. (2014) *The benefits of tackling worklessness and low pay*, York: Joseph Rowntree Foundation.

[37] Gardiner, L. and Wilson, T. (2012) *Hidden talents*, London: Local Government Association.

[38] IPPR North (2011) 'Transport spend per head is £2,700 for London but £5 per head in North East', available at http://www.ippr.org/news-and-media/press-releases/transport-spend-per-head-is-p2700-for-london-but-p5-per-head-in-north-east.

[39] Watmore, I. (2015) *A word on machinery of government changes – from a man who knows*, UK: Institute for Government.

[40] National Audit Office (2010) *Reorganising central government*, London: The Stationery Office.

[41] Timmins, N. (2012) *Never again? The story of the Health and Social Care Act 2012*, London: Institute for Government.

[42] Fleming, N. (2004) 'Bill for hi-tech NHS soars to £20 billion', *Daily Telegraph*, 10 December 2004, available at http://www.telegraph.co.uk/news/uknews/1473927/Bill-for-hi-tech-NHS-soars-to-20-billion.html.

[43] Dixon, A. et al (2010) *Patient choice*, UK: The King's Fund.

[44] Griffith, M. (2011) *We must fix it*, London: IPPR, p 14.

[45] Soffel, J. (2013) 'Rio's "big brother" control room watches over the city', CNN, available at http://edition.cnn.com/2013/08/29/world/americas/rio-big-brother-control-room/.

Three: The localist renaissance: how England's cities fought back

[1] Helprin, M. (1983) *Winter's tale*, US: Houghton Mifflin Harcourt.

[2] Stockport's Sue Derbyshire was represented by her deputy, Iain Roberts.

[3] Blond, P. and Morrin, M. (2014) *Devo max – devo manc*, London: Res Publica.

[4] The best history of Manchester's rejuvenation is undoubtedly Ray King's (2006) *Detonation: Rebirth of a city*, which I have drawn upon extensively in framing my understanding of the city.

[5] Quilley, S. (2002) 'Entrepreneurial turns: municipal socialism and after', in J. Peck and K. Ward (eds) *City of revolution: Restructuring Manchester*, Manchester: Manchester University Press.

[6] Agglomeration economics officially became part of the city's approach as part of the Manchester Independent Economic Review, which informs this section of the book. It can be downloaded at http://www.manchester-review.org.uk/.

[7] Pidd, H. (2014) 'Manchester metrolink line opens more than a year ahead of schedule', *Guardian*, available at http://www.theguardian.com/uk-news/2014/nov/02/manchester-metrolink-line-opens-ahead-schedule.

[8] Office for Budget Responsibility (2014) *Fiscal sustainability report*, London: The Stationery Office.

[9] Frey, C.B. and Osborne, M.A. (2013) 'The future of employment: How susceptible are jobs to computerisation?', available at http://www.oxfordmartin.ox.ac.uk/downloads/academic/The_Future_of_Employment.pdf.

[10] Rifkin, J. (2014) *The zero marginal cost society*, US: Palgrave Macmillan.

[11] Williams, D. (2015) *The flat white economy*, UK: Duckworth.

[12] Friedman, T. (2012) 'It's still half time in America', *New York Times*, available at http://www.nytimes.com/2012/09/02/opinion/sunday/friedman-its-still-halftime-in-america.html?ref=thomaslfriedman.

[13] Zimpher, N. (2012) 'A roadmap for education', *New York Times*, available at http://www.nytimes.com/2012/09/06/opinion/a-road-map-for-education.html?_r=0.

[14] Ernst and Young (2013) *Whole place community budgets: A review of the potential for aggregation*, London: Local Government Association.

[15] Kania, J. and Kramer, M. (2011) 'Collective impact', *Stanford Social Innovation Review*, available at http://www.ssireview.org/articles/entry/collective_impact; Bridgespan Group (2011) 'Case study: Cincinnati, Covington and Newport', available at http://www.bridgespan.org/getmedia/a01ac9cc-935e-4bdb-9401-fbb998512e44/Community-Collaboratives-CaseStudy-Cinncinnati.aspx, accessed on 16 March 2015; Geo (2012) 'Collaborative funding for greater impact: a case study of the Cincinnati experience', available at http://gosw.org/files/misc/sww_collab_funding_2012-1.pdf.

[16] The Economist (2014) 'The problem-solvers', available at http://www.economist.com/news/united-states/21618901-hints-how-provide-better-health-care-less-money-problem-solvers.

[17] Harrison, J.D. (2014) 'Maryland poaching start-ups left and right', *Washington Post*, available at http://www.washingtonpost.com/business/on-small-business/maryland-poaching-start-ups-left-and-right/2014/05/29/4f829b84-e76e-11e3-8f90-73e071f3d637_story.html.

[18] Alperovitz, G. (2012) 'New thinking for city finances', *Baltimore Sun*, available at http://www.baltimoresun.com/news/opinion/oped/bs-ed-cities-revenue-20120221-story.html.

[19] Manning, J. (2012) *More light, more power*, London: NLGN.

[20] Plunkett, J. (2011) *Growth without gain*, London: Resolution Foundation .

[21] Kenderdine, L. (2014) 'Council's low-interest shopping revolution', *Oldham Evening Chronicle*, 27 March 2014.

[22] Beresford, M. (2014) *Better business*, UK: Association for Public Service Excellence/NLGN.

[23] Beresford, M. (2014).

[24] Keohane, N. (2011) *Changing behaviours*, London: NLGN.

[25] iMPOWER Consulting (2012) 'Changing the game', available at: http://www.impower.co.uk/wp-content/uploads/impowerchangingthegame.pdf.

[26] Quoted in Schell, E. (2014) 'The creativity bubble', *Jacobin*, issue 15/16, available at https://www.jacobinmag.com/2014/10/the-creativity-bubble/.

Four: From consumers to creators: reinventing citizenship from the ground up

[1] MacLeod, K. (2013) *The star fraction*, UK: Tom Doherty Associates.

[2] See, for instance: http://www.theguardian.com/books/2012/dec/10/uk-lost-200-libraries-2012.

[3] Kuznetsova, D. and Symons, T. (2011) *Transforming universal services*, London: NLGN.

[4] Shared Intelligence (2014) 'Enterprising libraries: the waiting room', Carnegie UK Trust, available at http://www.carnegieuktrust.org.uk/CMSPages/GetFile.aspx?guid=d2b7d075–6b9a-4939-b9f3–2b20ebb18ca4, and Naylor, A. (2013) 'On the origins of St Botolphs', available at http://commonfutures.eu/wp-content/uploads/2013/11/On-the-Origins-of-St-Botolphs.pdf.

[5] Gregory, D. (2014) 'There is no such thing as capitalism', *Stir* magazine, Autumn 2014.

[6] Wall, D. (2014) 'Elinor Ostrom, the commons and anti-capitalism', *Stir* magazine, Winter 2014.

[7] See, for instance, Ostrom, E. (2009) 'Beyond markets and states: polycentric governance of complex economic systems', Nobel Prize for Economics lecture, 8 December 2009.

[8] Ipsos MORI (nd) 'Generations: pride in the welfare state', available at http://www.ipsos-mori-generations.com/Pride-in-welfare-state.

[9] Cited in Bollier, D. and Helfrich, S. (eds) *The wealth of the commons*, Massachusetts: Levellers Press.

[10] Co-operatives UK (2014) 'The UK Co-operative economy 2014', available at http://www.uk.coop/sites/storage/public/downloads/co-operative_economy_2014.pdf.

[11] Civic Systems Lab (2011) *Compendium for the civic economy*, London: 00:/.

[12] Swade, K., Simmonds, M. et al (2013) *Woodland social enterprise in England: data baseline*, London: Shared Assets.

[13] Ipsos MORI (2010b) poll for *The Economist*, available at https://www.ipsos-mori.com/Assets/Docs/Polls/poll-public-policy-poll-for-the-economist-may2010-charts.pdf, accessed on 17 March 15.

[14] Civil Exchange (2015) *Whose society? The final big society audit*, UK: Civil Exchange.

[15] Rauch, D. and Schleicher, D. (2015) 'Like Uber, but for local government policy', *George Mason Law & Economics Research Paper* No. 15-01, available at http://papers.ssrn.com/sol3/papers.cfm?abstract_id=2549919#%23.

[16] Boyle, D. and Bird, S. (2014) *Give and take: How timebanking is transforming healthcare*, Great Britain: Timebanking UK.

[17] Ambinder, E. and Jennings, D. (2013) *The resilient social network*, US: Department of Homeland Security.

[18] Solnit, R. (2009) *A paradise built in hell: The extraordinary communities that arise in disaster*, US: Penguin.

[19] Feuer, A. (2012) 'Occupy Sandy: a movement moves to relief', *New York Times*, 9 November 2012.

[20] Iaione, C. (2009) 'The tragedy of urban roads: saving cities from choking, calling on citizens to combat climate change', *Fordham Urban Law Journal*, vol 37, no 3, http://ir.lawnet.fordham.edu/ulj/vol37/iss3/7.

[21] Labgov (2014) 'Regulation on collaboration between citizens and the city for the care and regeneration of urban commons', available at http://www.comune.bologna.it/media/files/bolognaregulation.pdf, accessed on 17 March 2015.

[22] See, for instance, the Struggles Made in Italy blog, https://strugglesinitaly.wordpress.com/2013/12/30/en-social-streets-and-the-mutual-aid-economy/.

[23] Crouch, C. (2004) *Post-democracy*, UK: Wiley.

[24] Copus, C. (2004) *Party politics and local government*, Manchester: Manchester University Press.

[25] Sweeting, D. and Copus, C. (2012) 'Whatever happened to local democracy?', *Policy & Politics*, vol 40, no 1, pp 21–38.

[26] Rama, E. (2012) 'Take your city back with paint', talk to TedxThessaloniki, available at: https://www.ted.com/talks/edi_rama_take_back_your_city_with_paint?language=en.

Five: The colonisation of Britain: how the empire came home

[1] The Bermondsey case study is heavily based on Goss, S. (2013) 'A new Jerusalem: health services in Bermondsey', in S. Parker and J. Manning (eds) *The history boys*, London: NLGN; Municipal Dreams (2013a) 'The beautification of Bermondsey', available at https://municipaldreams.wordpress.com/2013/04/23/the-beautification-of-bermondsey-fresh-air-and-fun/, (2013b) 'Bermondsey's health education campaign: there is no wealth but life', available at https://municipaldreams.wordpress.com/2013/01/22/bermondseys-health-education-campaign-there-is-no-wealth-but-life/, and (2013c) 'Healthcare in Bermondsey: reaching for the new Jerusalem', available at: https://municipaldreams.wordpress.com/2013/09/10/1569/, all accessed on 16 March 15.

[2] White, J. (2004) 'From Herbert Morrison to command and control: the decline of local democracy', *History and Policy*, available at http://www.historyandpolicy. org/policy-papers/papers/from-herbert-morrison-to-command-and-control-the-decline-of-local-democracy.

[3] The statue has since been replaced, with money from the council and a public fund-raising campaign.

[4] See, for instance, Szreter, S. (2002) 'A central role for local government? The example of late Victorian Britain', *History and Policy*, available at http://www.historyandpolicy.org/policy-papers/papers/a-central-role-for-local-government-the-example-of-late-victorian-britain and Hunt, T. (2005) *Building Jerusalem: The rise and fall of the Victorian city*, Great Britain: Phoenix.

[5] Hennock, E.P. (1982) 'Central/local government relations in England: an outline 1800–1950', *Urban History*, vol 9, pp 38–49.

[6] Bulpitt, J. (1983) *Territory and power in the United Kingdom*, Manchester: University of Manchester Press.

[7] Webb, S. and Webb, B. (1975) *A constitution for the socialist commonwealth of Great Britain,* Cambridge: Cambridge University Press.

[8] Klein, R. (2010) *The new politics of the NHS* (6th edn), Oxford: Radcliffe Publishing.

[9] Timmins, N. (1996) *The five giants,* Great Britain: Fontana.

[10] Klein (2010).

[11] Hutchinson, G. (1950) 'The politicians reply', *Municipal Journal*, 6 January 1950.

[12] *Municipal Journal*, 'Notes and comments: changes are coming', 4 October 1946.

[13] *Municipal Journal*, 'Peckham: finance beats "greatest social venture"', 10 March 1950.

[14] Francis, M. (1997) *Ideas and policies under Labour, 1945–1951*, Manchester: Manchester University Press, p 50.

[15] Francis (1997), p 50.

[16] Crossman, R.H.S. (1956) *Socialism and the new despotism*, Great Britain: Fabian Society.

[17] Klein (2010).

[18] Bennett, A., writing in *Local Government Chronicle* Anniversary Supplement, 2 November 2005.

[19] Jackman, R. (1985) 'Local government finance', in M. Loughlin et al (eds) *Half a century of municipal decline*, Chatham: George Allen & Unwin.

[20] Bevan, A. (1946) 'My appeal to you', *Municipal Journal*, 19 July.

[21] Kynaston, D. (2014) *Modernity Britain book two: A shake of the dice 1959–62*, Great Britain: Bloomsbury.

[22] Benn, T. (1979) *Arguments for socialism*, Harmondsworth: Penguin.

[23] Davis-Coleman, C. (1985) 'Kinnock and Blunkett strive for unity – but divisions remain', *Municipal Journal*, 8 March 1985.

[24] McSmith, A. (1997) *Faces of Labour*, Great Britain: Verso, p 169.

[25] Butler, D., Adonis, A. et al (1994) *Failure in British government: The politics of the poll tax*, Oxford: Oxford University Press, p 28.

[26] Deakin, N. (1985) 'Local government and social policy', in *Half a century of municipal decline*, Chatham: George Allen & Unwin.

[27] Regan, D. (1987) *The local Left and its national pretensions*, London: Centre for Policy Studies.

[28] Barber, M. (2008) *Instruction to deliver*, Great Britain: Methuen.

[29] Hood, C. (2006) 'Gaming in Targetworld: the targets approach to managing British public services', *Public Administration Review*, July/August 2006.

[30] Blair, T. (2010) 'The importance of governance in the modern world', speech, Institute for Government.

[31] Department of Health (2009) 'Statement on contraception and teenage pregnancy', available at: http://webarchive.nationalarchives.gov.uk/+/www.dh.gov.uk/en/publichealth/healthimprovement/sexualhealth/DH_085686.

[32] 6, P. et al. (2010) 'Making people more responsible: the Blair governments' programme for changing citizen behaviour', *Political Studies, vol* 58, no 3, pp 427–49.

[33] Heseltine, M. (2012) *No stone unturned in pursuit of growth*, London: Her Majesty's Government.

[34] Mouritzen, P.E. (2012) 'On the (blessed) deficiencies of Danish democracy', in J. Blom-Hansen, C. Green-Pedersen, and S-E. Skaaning (eds), *Democracy, elections and political parties: Essays in honor of Jørgen Elklit*, Aarhus: Forlaget Politica, pp 181–92.

Six: Giving up is hard to do: why politicians struggle to share power

[1] Civil Exchange (2015) *Whose society? The final big society audit*, UK: Civil Exchange.

[2] Runciman, W.G. (2015) *Very different, but much the same*, Oxford: Oxford University Press.

[3] IPPR/PWC (2011) *Who's accountable? The challenge of giving power away in a centralised political culture*, London: IPPR.

[4] Gash,T., Randall,J. et al (2014) *Achieving political decentralisation*, London: Institute for Government.

[5] Gash, Randall et al (2014), and Bochel, H., Denver, D. et al (2013) *Scotland decides: The devolution issue and the 1997 referendum*, Abingdon: Routledge.

[6] Rutter, J., Marshall, E. et al (2012) *The 'S' factors*, London: Institute for Government.

[7] IPPR/PWC (2011).

[8] Gash, Randall et al (2014), and Pimlott, B. and Rao, N. (2002) *Governing London*, Oxford: Oxford University Press.

[9] Parker, S. (2011) 'Assessing the local authority mayors outside London', in T. Gash and S. Sims (eds) *What can elected mayors do for our cities?*, UK: Institute for Government.

Seven: Hack the state: how we can take power back

[1] Trocchi, A. (1963) A revolutionary proposal: Invisible insurrection of a million minds, Paris: International Situationiste.

[2] I wish I could claim credit for this chart and the idea it encapsulates, but it is actually borrowed and adapted from the blogger Adil Abrar, who coined the term 'peak state' in 2010 and explains it here: http://www.sidekickstudios. net/blog/2010/06/peak-state-and-the-valley-of-nobody-knows.

[3] See, for instance, Perez, C. (2013) 'Unleashing a golden age after the financial collapse: drawing lessons from history', *Environmental Innovations and Societal Transitions,* vol 6, March, pp 9–23.

[4] Dolphin, T. (2013) *A job for everyone*, London: IPPR.

[5] Ben-Galim, D. (2011) *Making the case for universal childcare*, London: IPPR.

[6] Citizens Income Trust (2012) 'Citizens income: an introduction', available at http://www.citizensincome.org/filelibrary/poster2013.pdf, accessed on 23 March 2015.

[7] Hirsch, D. (2015) *Could a 'citizen's income' work?*, York: Joseph Rowntree Foundation.

[8] O'Leary, D. (2014) 'What's mine is yours', *Demos Quarterly*, available at http:// quarterly.demos.co.uk/article/issue-2/skin-in-the-game/, accessed on 9 April 2015.

[9] I am currently involved in developing this approach in conjunction with 00 Research and Lend Lease.

[10] Haldenby, A., Harries, R. et al (2014) *Markets for good*, Great Britain: Reform.

[11] A version of this idea has been substantially developed by Matthew Pike and the Public Services Transformation Network and is likely to be trialled in 2016. I am indebted to Matthew for his help with this section of the book.

[12] Bjarnason, R. (2014) 'Your priorities: an Icelandic story of e-democracy', available at: http://communityboostr.org/news/your-priorities-icelandic-story-e-democracy.

[13] Ironically, it was vetoed by Herbert Morrison, the champion of local democracy.

References

6, P. et al (2010) 'Making people more responsible: the Blair governments' programme for changing citizen behaviour', *Political Studies, vol* 58, no 3, pp 427–49.

Alperovitz, G. (2012) 'New thinking for city finances', *Baltimore Sun*, available at http://www.baltimoresun.com/news/opinion/oped/bs-ed-cities-revenue-20120221-story.html.

Ambinder, E. and Jennings, D. (2013) *The Resilient Social Network*, US: Department of Homeland Security.

APPG on Primary Care and Public Health (2012) 'Ten years on from Wanless, how "fully engaged" are we?', available at http://www.pagb.co.uk/appg/inquiryreports/WanlessReview10yearson_2012.pdf.

Bakunin, M. (1867/1981) 'Federalism, socialism, anti-theologism' in S. Dolgoff (ed) *Bakunin on Anarchism*, Montreal.

Barber, M. (2008) *Instruction to deliver*, London: Methuen.

Ben-Galim, D. (2011) *Making the case for universal childcare*, London: Institute for Publish Policy Research.

Benn, T. (1979) *Arguments for socialism*, Harmondsworth: Penguin.

Beresford, M. (2014) *Better business*, UK: Association for Public Service Excellence/NLGN.

Bevan, A. (1946) 'My appeal to you', *Municipal Journal*, 19 July.

Bivand, P. and Simmons, D. (2014) *The benefits of tackling worklessness and low pay*, York: Joseph Rowntree Foundation .

Bjarnason, R. (2014) 'Your priorities: An Icelandic story of e-democracy', available at: http://communityboostr.org/news/your-priorities-icelandic-story-e-democracy.

Blair, T. (2010) 'The importance of governance in the modern world', speech, Institute for Government.

Blöchliger, H. (2013) 'Decentralisation and economic growth – Part 1: How fiscal federalism affects long-term development', *OECD Working Papers on Fiscal Federalism*, No 14, OECD Publishing.

Blond, P. and Morrin, M. (2014) *Devo max – devo manc*, London: Res Publica.

Blunkett, D. (2002) 'Responsibility without power: the worst of all worlds', excerpts available at: http://www.theguardian.com/society/2002/feb/01/publicservices.

Bochel, H., Denver, D. et al (2013) *Scotland decides: The devolution issue and the 1997 Referendum*, Abingdon: Routledge.

Bollier, D. and Helfrich, S. (eds) (2012) *The wealth of the commons*, Massachusetts: Levellers Press.

Boyle, D. and Bird, S. (2014) *Give and take: How timebanking is transforming healthcare*, Great Britain: Timebanking UK.

Bridgespan Group (2011) 'Case study: Cincinnati, Covington and Newport', available at http://www.bridgespan.org/getmedia/a01ac9cc-935e-4bdb-9401-fbb998512e44/Community-Collaboratives-CaseStudy-Cinncinnati.aspx.

Bullock, S. (2014) 'Local government and the NHS', in E. Burnell (ed) *Labour's local offer*, London: NLGN.

Bulpitt, J. (1983) *Territory and power in the United Kingdom*, Manchester: Manchester University Press.

Butler, D., Adonis, A. et al (1994) *Failure in British government: The politics of the poll tax*, Oxford: Oxford University Press, p 28.

Carswell, D. (2011) 'Politics will be dominated by those with ideas to disperse power', available at http://www.talkcarswell.com/home/politics-will-be-dominated-by-those-with-ideas/2021.

Castells, M. (2009) *Communication power*, Oxford and New York: Oxford University Press.

Chapman, J. (2015) 'Tough talk on bins exposed as rubbish after NO councils sign up to £250 million fund to restore weekly collections', *Daily Mail*, available at http://www.dailymail.co.uk/news/article-2908907/Pickles-bins-collection-fund-weekly-rounds-used-zero-councils-authority-considered-decided-expensive.html.

Citizens Income Trust (2012) 'Citizens income: an introduction', available at http://www.citizensincome.org/filelibrary/poster2013.pdf.

City Growth Commission (2014) *Unlocking metro growth*, London: RSA.

Civic Systems Lab (2011) *Compendium for the civic economy*, London: 00.

Civil Exchange (2015) *Whose society? The final Big Society audit*, UK: Civil Exchange.

Clark, G. (2012) *Decentralisation: An assessment of progress*, London: DCLG .

Co-operatives UK (2014) *The UK co-operative economy 2014*, available at http://www.uk.coop/sites/storage/public/downloads/co-operative_economy_2014.pdf.

Copus, C. (2004) *Party politics and local government*, Manchester: Manchester University Press.

Cottam, H. and James, R. (2014) *The life programme: A report on our work*, London: Participle.

Cristina Caballero, M. (2004) 'Academic turns city into a social experiment', *Harvard University Gazette*.

Crossman, R.H.S. (1956) *Socialism and the new despotism*, Great Britain: Fabian Society.

Crouch, C. (2004) *Post-democracy*, UK: Wiley.

Dalsgard, A. (director) (2012) 'Improving civic behaviour – cities on speed', available at https://www.youtube.com/watch?v=bwgWM3h_l-4.

Davis-Coleman, C. (1985) 'Kinnock and Blunkett strive for unity – but divisions remain', *Municipal Journal*, 8 March.

Deakin, N. (1985) 'Local government and social policy', in *Half a century of municipal decline,* Chatham: George Allen & Unwin, pp 202-31.

Department of Health (2009) 'Statement on contraception and teenage pregnancy', available at : http://webarchive.nationalarchives.gov.uk/+/www.dh.gov.uk/en/publichealth/healthimprovement/sexualhealth/DH_085686.

Dixon, A., Robertson, R. et al (2010) *Patient choice*, UK: The King's Fund.

Dolphin, T. (2013) *A job for everyone*, London: IPPR.

DWP/DfE (2012) *Child poverty in the UK: The report on the 2010 target*, London: The Stationery Office.

Ernst and Young (2013) *Whole place community budgets: A review of the potential for aggregation*, London: Local Government Association.

Feuer, A. (2012) 'Occupy Sandy: a movement moves to relief', *New York Times*, 9 November.

Francis, M. (1997) *Ideas and policies under Labour, 1945–1951*, Manchester: Manchester University Press, p 50.

Freeguard, G., Munro, R. et al (2015) *Whitehall monitor: Deep impact?*, London: Institute for Government.

Frey, C.B. and Osborne, M.A. (2013) 'The future of employment: how susceptible are jobs to computerisation?', available at http://www.oxfordmartin.ox.ac.uk/downloads/academic/The_Future_of_Employment.pdf.

Friedman, T. (2012) 'It's still half time in America', *New York Times*, available at http://www.nytimes.com/2012/09/02/opinion/sunday/friedman-its-still-halftime-in-america.html?ref=thomaslfriedman.

Gardiner, L. and Wilson, T. (2012) *Hidden talents*, London: Local Government Association.

Gash, T., Randall, J. et al (2014) *Achieving political decentralisation*, London: Institute for Government.

Geo (Grantmakers for Effective Organizations) (2012) 'Collaborative funding for greater impact: a case study of the Cincinnati experience', available at http://gosw.org/files/misc/sww_collab_funding_2012–1.pdf.

Goss, S. (2013) 'A new Jerusalem: health services in Bermondsey', in S. Parker and J. Manning (eds) *The history boys*, London: NLGN, pp 39-45.

Greer, S. (2010) 'Options and the lack of options: healthcare politics and policy', in V. Uberoi et al (eds) *Options for Britain II*, UK: Wiley-Blackwell, pp 39-45.

Gregory, D. (2014) 'There is no such thing as capitalism', *Stir* magazine, Autumn 2014.

Griffith, M. (2011) *We must fix it*, London: IPPR

Haldenby, A., Harries, R. et al (2014) *Markets for good*, Great Britain: Reform.

Harrison, J.D. (2014) 'Maryland poaching start-ups left and right', *Washington Post*, available at http://www.washingtonpost.com/business/on-small-business/maryland-poaching-start-ups-left-and-right/2014/05/29/4f829b84-e76e-11e3-8f90-73e071f3d637_story.html.

Heath, S. (2014) *Housing demand and need (England)*, UK: House of Commons Library.

Heimans, J. and Timms, H. (2014) 'Understanding new power', *Harvard Business Review*, available at https://hbr.org/2014/12/understanding-new-power.

Helprin, M. (1983) *Winter's tale*, US: Houghton Mifflin Harcourt.

Hennock, E.P. (1982) 'Central/local government relations in England: an outline 1800–1950', *Urban History*, vol 9, pp 38–49.

Heseltine, M. (2012) *No stone unturned in search of growth*, London: Her Majesty's Government.

Hirsch, D. (2015) *Could a 'citizen's income' work?*, York: Joseph Rowntree Foundation.

Hood, C. (2006) 'Gaming in Targetworld: the targets approach to managing British public services', *Public Administration Review*, July/August 2006.

Hunt, T. (2005) *Building Jerusalem: The rise and fall of the Victorian city*, Great Britain: Phoenix.

Hutchinson, G. (1950) 'The politicians reply', *Municipal Journal*, 6 January.

Iaione, C. (2009) 'The tragedy of urban roads: Saving cities from choking, calling on citizens to combat climate change', *Fordham Urban Law Journal*, vol 37, no 3, pp 890-951.

Ilich, I. (1971) *Deschooling society*, New York: Harper and Row.

iMPOWER Consulting (2012) *Changing the game*, available at: http://www.impower.co.uk/wp-content/uploads/impowerchangingthegame.pdf.

IPPR/PWC (2011) *Who's accountable? The challenge of giving power away in a centralised political culture*, London: Institute for Public Policy Research.

IPPR North (2011) 'Transport spend per head is £2,700 for London but £5 per head in North East', available at http://www.ippr.org/news-and-media/press-releases/transport-spend-per-head-is-p2700-for-london-but-p5-per-head-in-north-east.

Ipsos MORI (nd) 'Generations: pride in the welfare state', available at http://www.ipsos-mori-generations.com/Pride-in-welfare-state, accessed 17 March 2015.

Ipsos MORI (2010a) *What do people want, need and expect from public services?*, London: RSA.

Ipsos Mori (2010b) poll for *The Economist*, available at https://www. ipsos-mori.com/Assets/Docs/Polls/poll-public-policy-poll-for-the-economist-may2010-charts.pdf.

Ipsos MORI (2013) 'Leader perceptions poll', available at https://www. ipsos-mori.com/Assets/Docs/Polls/LeadershipPoll_topline.PDF.

Jackman, R. (1985) 'Local government finance', in M. Loughlin et al (eds) *Half a century of municipal decline*, Chatham: George Allen & Unwin.

Jenkins, S. (2004) *Big bang localism: A rescue plan for British democracy*, London: Policy Exchange.

Kania, J. and Kramer, M. (2011) 'Collective impact', *Stanford Social Innovation Review*, available at http://www.ssireview.org/articles/entry/collective_impact.

Kenderdine, L. (2014) 'Council's low-interest shopping revolution', *Oldham Evening Chronicle*, 27 March.

Keohane, N. (2011) *Changing behaviours*, London: NLGN.

King, A. and Crewe, I. (2013) *The blunders of our governments*, Oxford: Oneworld Publications.

King, R. (2006) *Detonation: Rebirth of a city*, Great Britain: Clear Publications Limited.

Klein, R. (2010) *The new politics of the NHS* (6th edn), Oxford: Radcliffe Publishing.

Kuznetsova, D. and Symons, T. (2011) *Transforming universal services*, London: NLGN.

Kynaston, D. (2014) *Modernity Britain: Book Two: A shake of the dice 1959–62*, Great Britain: Bloomsbury.

Labgov (2014) 'Regulation on collaboration between citizens and the city for the care and regeneration of urban commons', available at http://www.comune.bologna.it/media/files/bolognaregulation.pdf.

McGovern, A. (2015) 'Labour's unfinished business: The children still living in poverty', *New Statesman*, available at http://www. newstatesman.com/politics/2015/02/labours-unfinished-business-children-still-living-poverty.

MacLeod, K. (2013) *The star fraction*, UK: Tom Doherty Associates.

McSmith, A. (1997) *Faces of Labour*, London: Verso.

Manning, J. (2012) *More light, more power*, London: NLGN.

Marmot, M. (2014) 'Foreword', in *If you could change one thing*, London: British Academy.

Matheson, G. (2014) *Speech by Councillor Gordon Matheson*, available at https://www.glasgow.gov.uk/index.aspx?articleid=14319.

Monitor (2013) 'Closing the NHS funding gap: how to get better value healthcare for patients', available at https://www.gov.uk/government/uploads/system/uploads/attachment_data/file/284044/ClosingTheGap091013.pdf.

Morris, W. (1908) *News from nowhere*, London: Longmans.

Mouritzen, P.E. (2012) 'On the (blessed) deficiencies of Danish democracy', in J. Blom-Hansen, C. Green-Pedersen, and S-E. Skaaning (eds) *Democracy, elections and political parties: Essays in honor of Jørgen Elklit*, Aarhus: Forlaget Politica, pp 181–92.

Municipal Dreams (2013a) 'The beautification of Bermondsey', available at https://municipaldreams.wordpress.com/2013/04/23/the-beautification-of-bermondsey-fresh-air-and-fun/.

Municipal Dreams (2013b) 'Bermondsey's health education campaign: there is no wealth but life', available at https://municipaldreams.wordpress.com/2013/01/22/bermondseys-health-education-campaign-there-is-no-wealth-but-life/.

Municipal Dreams (2013c) 'Healthcare in Bermondsey: reaching for the new Jerusalem', available at: https://municipaldreams.wordpress.com/2013/09/10/1569/.

Municipal Dreams (2014) 'The Hulme Crescents, Manchester: bringing "a touch of 18th century grace and dignity" to municipal building', available at: https://municipaldreams.wordpress.com/2014/03/04/the-hulme-crescents-manchester-bringing-a-touch-of-eighteenth-century-grace-and-dignity-to-municipal-building/.

Municipal Journal (1946) 'Notes and comments: changes are coming', 4 October.

Municipal Journal (1950) 'Peckham: finance beats "greatest social venture"', 10 March.

Natcen Social Research (2014) *British Social Attitudes: 31st edition*, Greater Britain: Natcen.

National Audit Office (2010) *Reorganising central government*, London: The Stationery Office.

Naylor, A. (2013) 'On the origins of St Botolphs', available at http://commonfutures.eu/wp-content/uploads/2013/11/On-the-Origins-of-St-Botolphs.pdf.

NHS England (2013a) 'High quality care for all, now and for future generations', available at http://www.england.nhs.uk/wp-content/uploads/2013/06/urg-emerg-care-ev-bse.pdf.

NHS England (2013b) 'The NHS belongs to the people: a call to action', available at www.england.nhs.uk/wp-content/uploads/2013/07/nhs_belongs.pdf.

NHS England (2014) 'Get serious about obesity or bankrupt the NHS', available at http://www.england.nhs.uk/2014/09/17/serious-about-obesity/, accessed on 17 March 2015.

OECD (2010) 'A family affair: intergenerational social mobility across OECD countries', in *Going for Growth*, Paris: OECD.

OECD (2013) *Government at a glance*, Paris: OECD.

Office for Budget Responsibility (2014) *Welfare trends report*, London: The Stationery Office.

Office of National Statistics (2009) 'Housing', in *Social trends 39*, Houndmills: Palgrave Macmillan, chapter 10.

O'Leary, D. (2014) 'What's mine is yours', *Demos Quarterly*, available at http://quarterly.demos.co.uk/article/issue-2/skin-in-the-game/.

Ostrom, E. (2009) 'Beyond markets and states: polycentric governance of complex economic systems', Nobel Economics Prize lecture, 8 December 2009.

Parker, S. (2011) 'Assessing the local authority mayors outside London', in T. Gash and S. Sims (eds) *What can elected mayors do for our cities?*, London: Institute for Government.

Parker, S. and Hallsworth, M. (2010) *What makes a 'successful' policy?*, London: Institute for Government.

Parker, S., Paun, A. et al (2010) *State of the service*, London: Institute for Government .

Perez, C. (2013) 'Unleashing a golden age after the financial collapse: drawing lessons from history', *Environmental Innovations and Societal Transitions,* vol 6, March, pp 9–23.

Pettit, P. (1997) *Republicanism*, Oxford: Oxford University Press.

Pidd, H. (2014) 'Manchester Metrolink line opens more than a year ahead of schedule', *Guardian*, available at http://www.theguardian.com/uk-news/2014/nov/02/manchester-metrolink-line-opens-ahead-schedule.

Pimlott, B. and Rao, N. (2002) *Governing London*, Oxford: Oxford University Press.

Plunkett, J. (2011) *Growth without gain*, London: Resolution Foundation.

Powell, H. (2013) 'Local engagement and raising public confidence – what do the public think?,' available at https://www.ipsos-mori.com/Assets/Docs/News/helen-powell-pcc-conference-policing-2013.pdf.

Prince, R. (2011) 'Eric Pickles: public will lose faith in councils which fail to collect bins', *Daily Telegraph*, available at http://www.telegraph.co.uk/news/politics/conservative/8283779/Eric-Pickles-public-will-lose-faith-in-councils-which-fail-to-collect-bins.html, accessed on 17 March 2015.

Quilley, S. (2002) 'Entrepreneurial turns: municipal socialism and after', in J. Peck and K. Ward (eds) *City of revolution: Restructuring Manchester*, Manchester: Manchester University Press, pp 76-94.

Rama, E. (2012) 'Take your city back with paint', talk to TedxThessaloniki, available at: https://www.ted.com/talks/edi_rama_take_back_your_city_with_paint?language=en.

Rauch, D. and Schleicher, D. (2015) 'Like Uber, but for local government policy', George Mason Law and Economics Research Paper No 15-01, available at http://papers.ssrn.com/sol3/papers.cfm?abstract_id=2549919#%23.

Regan, D. (1987) *The local Left and its national pretensions*, London: Centre for Policy Studies .

Ridley, N. (1988) *The local Right*, Mitcham: Centre for Policy Studies.

Rifkin, J. (2014) *The zero marginal cost society*, US: Palgrave Macmillan.

Royal College of Surgeons (2014) 'Is access to surgery a postcode lottery?', available at: http://www.rcseng.ac.uk/news/docs/Is%20access%20to%20surgery%20a%20postcode%20lottery.pdf.

Runciman, W.G. (2015) *Very different, but much the same*, Oxford: Oxford University Press.

Rushe, D. (2014) 'Is Uber the worst company in Silicon Valley?', Guardian, available at http://www.theguardian.com/technology/2014/nov/18/uber-worst-company-silicon-valley.

Rutter, J., Marshall, E. et al (2012) The 'S' factors, London: Institute for Government.

Saatchi, M. (2014) The road from serfdom, London: Centre for Policy Studies.

Schell, E. (2014) 'The creativity bubble', Jacobin, issue 15/16, available at https://www.jacobinmag.com/2014/10/the-creativity-bubble/.

Shared Intelligence (2014) 'Enterprising libraries: the waiting room', Carnegie UK Trust, available at http://www.carnegieuktrust.org.uk/CMSPages/GetFile.aspx?guid=d2b7d075–6b9a-4939-b9f3–2b20ebb18ca4.

Skinner, Q. (1997) Liberty before liberalism, Cambridge: Cambridge University Press.

Soffel, J. (2013) 'Rio's "big brother" control room watches over the city', CNN, available at http://edition.cnn.com/2013/08/29/world/americas/rio-big-brother-control-room/.

Solnit, R. (2009) A paradise built in hell: The extraordinary communities that arise in disaster, US: Penguin.

Swade, K., Simmonds, M. et al (2013) Woodland social enterprise in England: Data baseline, London: Shared Assets.

Sweeting, D. and Copus, C. (2012) 'Whatever happened to local democracy?', Policy & Politics, vol 40, no 1, pp 21–38.

Symons, T. and Rodriguez, L. (2011) Build to let, London: NLGN.

Szreter, S. (2002) 'A central role for local government? The example of late Victorian Britain', History and Policy, available at http://www.historyandpolicy.org/policy-papers/papers/a-central-role-for-local-government-the-example-of-late-victorian-britain.

Tawney, R.H. (1920) The acquisitive society, New York: Harcourt, Brace and Company .

Taylor-Gooby, P. (2006) 'The efficiency/trust dilemma', working paper, ESRC SCARR Network: Canterbury.

The Economist (2014) 'The problem-solvers', available at http://www.economist.com/news/united-states/21618901-hints-how-provide-better-health-care-less-money-problem-solvers.

Thomas, B., Dorling, D. et al (2010) 'Inequalities in premature mortality in Britain: observational study from 1921 to 2007', *British Medical Journal*, vol 341:c3639.

Timmins, N. (1996) *The five giants*, Great Britain: Fontana.

Timmins, N. (2012) *Never again? The story of the Health and Social Care Act 2012*, London: Institute for Government.

Tomaney, J., Pike, A. et al (2011) *Decentralisation outcomes: A review of evidence and analysis of international data*, London: DCLG.

Townsend, E. (2009) *UK income inequality and international comparisons*, London: House of Commons Library.

Trocchi, A. (1963) *A Revolutionary proposal: Invisible insurrection of a million minds*, Paris: International Situationiste.

Walker, D. (2002) 'Hold the centre', *Guardian*, available at http://www.theguardian.com/politics/2002/nov/21/budget2003.society.

Wall, D. (2014) 'Elinor Ostrom, the commons and anti-capitalism', *Stir* magazine, Winter.

Wanless, D. (2002) *Securing our future health: Taking a long term view*, London: Her Majesty's Treasury.

Webb, S. and Webb, B. (1975) *A constitution for the socialist commonwealth of Great Britain*, Cambridge: Cambridge University Press.

White, J. (2004) 'From Herbert Morrison to command and control: The decline of local democracy', *History and Policy*, available at http://www.historyandpolicy.org/policy-papers/papers/from-herbert-morrison-to-command-and-control-the-decline-of-local-democracy.

Williams, D. (2015) *The flat white economy*, UK: Duckworth.

Wilson, J. (2012) *Letting go*, UK: Fabian Society.

Zimpher, N. (2012) 'A roadmap for education', *New York Times*, available at http://www.nytimes.com/2012/09/06/opinion/a-road-map-for-education.html?_r=0.

Index

Page references for endnotes are followed by the note number, eg 156n13.

176 TAKING POWER BACK